New
Home

New Home

James Soane

For Christopher

First published in 2003
by Conran Octopus Limited,
a part of Octopus Publishing Group,
2–4 Heron Quays, London E14 4JP
www.conran-octopus.co.uk

Publishing Director: Lorraine Dickey
Senior Editor: Katey Day
Project Editor: Bridget Hopkinson
Art Director: Chi Lam
Designer: Lucy Gowans
Picture Research: Marissa Keating
Production Manager: Angela Couchman

British Cataloguing-in-Publication Data.
A catalogue record for this book is available from the British Library
ISBN 1 84091 283 9
Printed and bound in China

Contents

Foreword

Of all building types, houses and housing provide the greatest variety and the most complex history; as the first chapter of this storehouse of high-quality housing design puts it: 'from shelter to comfort'. At a time when an immense weight of media coverage is devoted to the house and home, these pages are a reminder that before makeovers, there are originals. Before the quest for originality comes precedent. And before precedent comes context.

Not the least fascinating aspect of the architecture of homes is the way in which different cultural, economic and social contexts produce parallel extremes of architecture and interior design. This is because architecture acts both as a sponge in respect of the influences that bring it into being, and as a reflector of the particular society in which it operates.

A complete analysis of any of the buildings in these pages would give you a mini-history of the society in which they were created, even though the examples are largely from the upper reaches of architectural thinking. This volume acts as a timely warning that speed, economy and process are by no means the only elements in the creation of that most civilized of concepts – the well-designed home.

Paul Finch

Introduction

In an age obsessed with image and lifestyle the idea of 'home' remains highly topical. At every turn, we are saturated with images showing us how and where to live, as well as which cars to drive and what clothes to wear. This collision of function, fashion and taste often blurs the distinction between fantasy and reality. The glossy publishing world spends a great deal of time polishing the surface, but rather less energy on asking more probing questions about the way we live now and the sorts of homes we wish to inhabit.

New Home seeks to examine the issues and debates currently surrounding the design of modern homes. No particular style or approach is shown to be more valid than another, but what does link each of the projects illustrated in these pages is the strength of the idea embedded at its heart. All take a different approach to solving the age-old problems of shelter, comfort and aesthetics in an innovative and unique way. Some houses are scarcely there at all, while others are constructions of a much grander ambition; many have been built with sustainability in mind, an evermore pressing consideration for architects and clients alike. Each project, though, should be a reminder that design is a creative process which can generate many different answers to the essentially unchanged question, How do I want to live?

Architecture has the power to inform the way we lead our daily lives and to transform the banality of the everyday. This is particularly true of the places we live in. To be able to commission a new house is a rare opportunity for most of us and people in this fortunate position often have strong ideas and desires concerning the homes they wish to create. Naturally these reflect their very specific requirements, be they for flexible accommodation in a busy city or for a rural Modernist retreat, but they can also be seen as representative of the culture as a whole. The challenges confronting contemporary architects, therefore, are not just practical and stylistic, they also have something to do with capturing the spirit of the here and now. The results are often inspiring architectural experiments that not only accommodate the dreams and concepts of the owners, but also engage with the wider world, serving as blueprints for future patterns of living.

1. From Shelter to Comfort

From Shelter to Comfort
History and Context

This chapter is by no means intended as a full historical survey of domestic architecture; rather, it is a collection of observations on the origins of that architecture and some of the ideas that have influenced the design of our own homes. The history that follows is based primarily on that of the West.

In today's fast moving, inter-connected world the merger of East and West, of opposite time zones, has been made possible through the advent of new technology. This global phenomenon has changed the way we all live and has opened up many exciting and challenging possibilities. Before the development of instant communication, progress was made at a much slower pace: local traditions were upheld for centuries and it was only the pioneers who travelled, and those who had the power to build monuments, who created landmarks in history, drawing on wider cultural references.

The history of architecture has often been told through 'great' buildings – churches, cathedrals, palaces and castles – and indeed these buildings were crucial to the development of towns and cities, and their individual identities. Yet the humble domestic house is often left out. This is not least because much domestic architecture was not

constructed from solid brick and stone but made of materials such as timber, mud and thatch, all of them more vulnerable to weathering and to catastrophic natural events. It is remarkable, then, that excellent examples of fifteenth-century domestic architecture still remain in rural Europe, and that homes dating back more than 800 years are still lived in, from Italian hill towns to Irish villages.

Another reason for the relative lack of attention given the everyday home is largely social; grand houses were for the ruling upper classes, while the lower classes and workers lived in modest accommodation that held little interest for the historians. It is important to note that in this book on the home, the realm of the 'household' is not examined, that is, the large house owned by a wealthy individual employing servants, cooks, gardeners and so on. These more ambitious constructions occupy a different territory to the one we explore here.

In one fundamental respect the concept of the house has altered very little over the past 2000 years; it is a place offering shelter. This very basic need has been culturally conditioned and over time the relationships between function, form and aesthetics have been redefined endlessly. It could be argued that the expression of 'home' at any one period of history is a good indicator of the social values of that time.

The ancient home Wandering around the streets of Pompeii, the Roman town that was buried under molten lava in AD 79, one can still sense the emotion of the place, almost hear children playing in the street, and certainly visualize what life was like under the blazing midday sun. In many ways it is not that different from the places we live in today.

Well over two thousand years ago, thriving cosmopolitan towns existed from Italy and Greece to the Middle East. All were settlements where people worked, lived and socialized. These communities had developed a sophisticated political status quo, allowing the gentry to enjoy the privileges of an urban existence while the majority worked to produce food, build infrastructure and maintain the town's fabric. The famous Roman architect and engineer Marcus Vitruvius Pollio makes a reference to houses of 'men with ordinary means' in the first century BC. It is no surprise to find that these were small rectangular houses with porches

Opposite above The Roman ruins at Pompeii in southern Italy, preserved by the volcanic ash that erupted from Mount Vesuvius in AD 79, give a strong impression of an elegant and ordered streetscape. Above The houses at Pompeii contained grand formal rooms that were richly decorated with frescoes that still survive.

or sometimes a small shop in the front room. Much of Rome's population lived in overcrowded tenements of several storeys that were built of mud-brick and timber. After the fire of AD 64, large parts of Rome were rebuilt on a system of straight, broad streets that formed rectangular blocks known as insulae, resulting in a model for urban planning that is still used today.

From archaeological findings at places like Pompeii a clear picture emerges of the kinds of houses more wealthy families inhabited. A fine example is the House of Surgeons, dating from 300 BC. Its modest entrance hall opens up on to an atrium that lets in light and rainwater. On two sides of this internal courtyard are open-plan bedrooms and at the far end a living space with views out on to a garden. Many houses were decorated inside with frescoes and mosaic floors which became increasingly decorative during the second and first centuries BC. In the cooler climate of Britain, Fishbourne, in West Sussex, dating from AD 75, was one of the first Roman residences with central heating. Many of the floors 'floated' above a void in which fires were lit. The hot air was drawn under the floors to heat whole rooms, sometimes through

double-thickness walls. The quality of life in these homes would have been luxurious even by today's standards and it is clear that the design of Roman dwellings could be highly sophisticated, and that issues of comfort and the enjoyment of ornament were elegantly resolved.

When the Romans' grip on Europe began to fail in the fifth century, with them went a whole way of life. The next 500 years of turmoil are known as the Dark Ages and it was not until greater political stability was achieved that domestic architecture truly flourished again.

Medieval merchant towns During the fourteenth and fifteenth centuries many towns and cities developed through the expansion of trade and an increasingly wealthy merchant class built dignified houses in these centres of commerce. An excellently preserved example of a medieval weaving town is that of Lavenham in Suffolk, England. Settled by Flemish weavers in 1380, the town grew to include an impressive collection of civic buildings, such as a guildhall, and many fine merchants' houses. These skilfully constructed houses are characterized by exposed timber frames, first floors that jut out to

Above Fishbourne Palace, in Sussex, England, has been excavated to reveal an innovatory hypocaust; beneath the occupied floor-level hot air was circulated to warm the rooms in an impressive feat of engineering and ingenuity.

maximize space (known as jetties) and leaded-glass windows. They were prefabricated as a series of frames which were lifted into position and pegged together. The panels were then infilled with wattle and daub (woven twigs covered with clay, water and straw) and painted with limewash to protect the timber. Many of the houses combined spaces for living and working: some had weaving lofts in the roofs, others had shop fronts. Records also describe lowlier 'tenements' which were rustic cottages with one or two rooms on the ground floor and a bedroom upstairs. There was no plumbing and, although there was a fire in the centre of the house, there was often no chimney, just a hole in the roof. Windows would not have held glass but could be closed using wooden shutters or blankets.

By way of contrast, in fifteenth-century Italy the prosperous city of Florence became the centre of an artistic Renaissance. The works of the great Roman and Greek writers were rediscovered and studied for the first time since the fall of Rome, and rich patrons such as the Medici family used their wealth to commission magnificent works from artists and architects. Notably in architecture, there was a revival of ancient rules and forms. Guided by the writing of the Roman author Vitruvius, Leon Battista Alberti introduced Roman columns and arches into his buildings. His imposing stone Palazzo Rucellai of 1457 was the first example of domestic architecture built in the Classical style which was to dominate this whole period of growth.

The spread of Classicism The growing populations of the fifteenth and sixteenth centuries began to change the character and density of the urban landscape. However it was the rise of Classicism in Europe during the seventeenth and eighteenth centuries that saw new forms in domestic architecture.

In England the uniformity of terraced housing allowed for more intense development and this type of townhouse is as relevant today as it was 400 years ago when it came into being. In London the square was developed as a model for organizing houses, a good example of which is St James's Square, begun in 1665. Here a small central park allows for intimate but public interaction as well as a view out on to nature. The houses are of uniform design and were therefore economical to build. This borrowing of Classical architecture continued into

Above Prentice Street in the historic town of Lavenham, in Suffolk, England, is a fine example of fifteenth-century timber construction. The houses are timber framed, infilled with lath and plaster, and are lived in to this day.

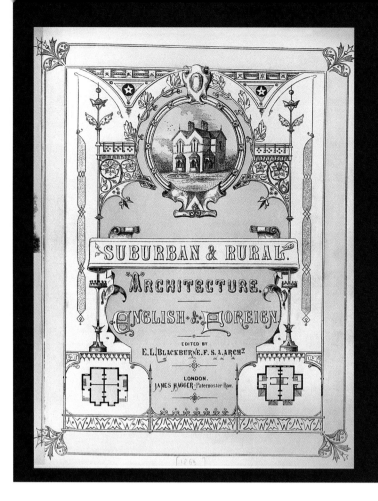

the eighteenth century and was employed to great effect by John Wood the Elder when he designed the Circus at Bath, England, which was completed in 1754. This grand circular terrace contains 33 townhouses and is unified by three orders of Doric columns which march across the curving construction. Interestingly, the houses themselves were erected by different builders after the main façade had been constructed, resulting in a more jumbled architectural expression behind the dignified frontage.

Architecture in the United States was also influenced by Classicism in the eighteenth century. Drayton Hall in South Carolina, completed in 1742 by John Drayton, displays some likeness to the villas of Andrea Palladio which were built in mid-sixteenth-century Italy. It is a well-proportioned, symmetrically fronted house that incorporates Classical columns and a temple-like roof. Thomas Jefferson, who became the third president of the United States, was also inspired by Palladio and in the 1770s designed his own house, Monticello, in Charlottesville, Virginia, to a Palladian model. As a distinguished amateur architect, Jefferson did much to popularize the Classical style in the United States.

Throughout this period American architects looked to the past for their inspiration, wishing to establish a dialogue with history and a cultural synthesis of Europe and the ancient world.

New patterns of living
The nineteenth century is arguably characterized by the rise of the middle classes. In the story of the development of the house this was important as the newly wealthy could afford to buy plots of land and build their own homes. By the 1840s established builders across Europe had what were known as housing pattern books, such as J C Loudon's *Encyclopaedia of Cottage, Farm and Villa Architecture*, first published in 1833, from which aspiring families could choose the designs of their residences. This led to a plethora of new styles of domestic architecture, from elegant townhouses to ornate suburban villas.

In the cities, property speculation was big business. In London the developer Thomas Cubitt was responsible for many of the terraces of houses and villas, such as those in Belgravia and Bloomsbury, that make up the inner suburbs and which became increasingly popular at the beginning of the Victorian period. As early as 1824 he designed houses in

Above Pattern books of house designs became increasingly popular in the nineteenth century. These collections of drawings and engravings showed a variety of plans and styles of execution ranging from Tudor and Venetian, to French Renaissance and even 'Hindu'.

Islington featuring double bay windows and their own water closets. Cheaper terraces were more basic, however, with outside lavatories at the backs of the houses. Such homes often had no entrance hall and one entered straight into the lounge or parlour from the street. In the two-storey version the building was often divided into two flats. The decoration of these basic houses was carried out by the builders and stained-glass windows, cornices and dadoes, and embossed wallpaper were all considered appropriate.

Also in the nineteenth century, the concept of 'suburbia' came into being. Huge swathes of housing for the better-off were developed away from the congested centres of the cities. This new way of living was made possible by improvements in mass transportation – in London, for example, the Underground system reached into Essex in the east and as far as Amersham in the northwest. The posters of the time have an innocent quality, showing the benefits for families of living with a garden in the unspoiled new estates. The houses were cheaper as well.

Elsewhere in Europe expanding city populations caused huge infrastructure and housing problems,

and new models of urban development were put into action. In Paris, working under Napoleon III, Baron Georges-Eugène Haussmann carried out impressive but controversial urban restructuring. He demolished slums, built new drainage systems and installed fresh-water supplies. He cut broad boulevards through the city, laid out public parks, created vast public monuments and built more bridges across the river Seine to ease congestion.

Art Nouveau The end of the nineteenth century saw the emergence of an exotic decorative style called Art Nouveau which was a celebration of natural forms. One of the most well-known houses of this period is the Hotel Tassel (1892) in Brussels designed by Victor Horta. Here the sensual obsession with nature is expressed in the intricate details of ironwork, wall paintings and mosaic. The botanical theme is taken from two dimensions to three as forms literally grow from surface decoration to become sculptural elements. While many found Art Nouveau appealing, many others considered it wilful, over-detailed and fanciful. There was a growing feeling among intellectual circles in Paris, Berlin, Brussels and Vienna that it represented

Above Victor Horta's Hotel Tassel is a homage to Art Nouveau. The wrought-iron staircase contains filigree detailing which reflects the painted decoration on the walls. On the outside, the balconies provide a layer of fine detail to the façade.

an indulgent *fin-de-siècle* lifestyle that was out of touch with reality. It can be argued that the design revolution of the twentieth century was a reaction to this florid stylistic movement. The preoccupation with ornament in this period resulted in a failure to fully develop new ideas about everyday dwellings. The new century, however, would be a time of progress and change, and this would be reflected in the houses people lived in.

A modern world It is curious how culture seems to respond to dates. Europe began to seem very different on the cusp of the nineteenth and twentieth centuries. In 1901 London saw the staging of the Great Exhibition, an attempt to capture some of the glamour and splendour of the Crystal Palace exhibition 50 years earlier. To many critics of the day, however, it was representative of an empire showing off, full of displays and spectacles to amuse rather than a showcase of social and technological progress or ideas for the future. Progress was inevitable, however, it was just a question of direction. As new infrastructures, factories and commercial buildings were constructed to meet the needs of industry, they inadvertently provided blueprints for a more

simple and rational architecture. In 1904 a vision of a modern Utopian city was presented by French architect Tony Garnier at the Ecole des Beaux-Arts in Paris. Here cubic residences stood in tree-lined boulevards, set away from administrative and cultural buildings which were sited in different zones. Garnier later named this layout 'An Industrial City'. The importance of his thoughts and drawings were not realized at the time, but they later became influential in the 1920s when architects such as Le Corbusier (see p.25) began to develop more definite proposals for a brave new world.

Tradition and decoration One of the favoured approaches to housing in Britain in the early twentieth century is epitomized by the domestic architecture of Sir Edwin Lutyens. He was a great believer in the Arts and Crafts Movement – which sought to reform design, and with it society, by the rediscovery of vernacular styles and craft skills – and drew on local references to inform his work. In 1901 he built Homewood, a house for his mother-in-law, in Knebworth. It is a large and elegantly proportioned four-square building sitting on a brick plinth, with extended, sloping tiled roofs

Above left The southwest façade of Homewood, built by Sir Edwin Lutyens in 1901, is characterized by two gabled roofs reminiscent of traditional farm houses. The composition is enhanced by the horizontal timber cladding separating the almost classical base.

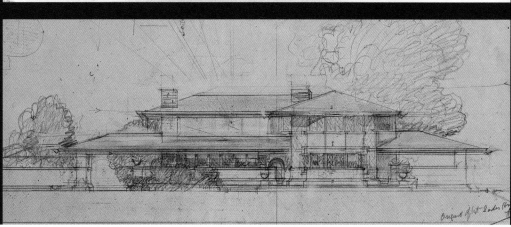

that refer to the local tradition of barn construction. Lutyens's building is by no means generic, however; his manipulation of the plan resulted in a superbly inventive cross-section, containing a grand, naturally lit stair right at the centre. This traditional language began to be seen as the appropriate style for the middle-class housing that was increasingly in demand in suburbia. Indeed Hampstead Garden Suburb in London, the centre of which was laid out by Lutyens, remains a seductive vision of a residential neighbourhood within a lush planted setting.

In the United States, the work of Frank Lloyd Wright also grew out of an admiration of local traditions and materials. Before the nineteenth century, architects had been seen not as professionals but as master-builders and craftsmen. Craftsmanship was key to the development of domestic architecture as traditional ways of making buildings were passed on from generation to generation. The tradition of craft building was very evident in the pared-down architecture of the Shakers, a sub-sect of the Quakers, who built their own communities of houses and churches in America in the eighteenth and nineteenth centuries. They believed that by living an ascetic life one could

Above The Shakers developed a restrained language of detailing and form which reflected an understanding of craftsmanship as well as the austere values of their society. They incorporated storage elements into the fabric of their homes, freeing them from clutter and unnecessary furniture.

come closer to God. Their domestic arrangements were very strict and are exquisitely reflected in their homes. The exteriors are of simple painted boarding while the interiors celebrate the craft of woodwork in beautifully turned banisters, precisely fitted wardrobes and long rows of hanging pegs. This stripped-down aesthetic appears 'minimalist' in today's terms, and in many ways it was. But it is the materiality of these places that transforms them from abstract compositions into warm and embracing homes.

Lloyd Wright embarked on his lifelong passion, to design good affordable housing, in the late 1880s. His 'Home for a Prairie Town' of 1901 illustrated a genteel, out-of-town existence. In 1909 he completed the Robie House in Chicago. This building owes a great deal to the classical vernacular of his 'prairie' houses, yet is also extraordinarily inventive. The composition of long horizontal planes is capped by overhanging, low-pitched roofs which give an appearance almost like that of a Japanese temple. This is not merely a coincidence: Wright was a great admirer of Japanese culture and went on to do some of his most important work in Tokyo. The house makes a feature of the walled forecourt,

another Asian element, and includes a built-in garage for three cars. The internal plan is laid out in such a way that the spaces seem to flow into one another. This approach to architecture appears ahead of its time: the collaging of different influences, the Japanese appreciation of boundaries and space, coupled with a keen interest in new building technologies, resulted in a hybrid building that was entirely new.

Natural forms In other places there were small pockets of a new, even more radical spirit. In Scotland Charles Rennie Mackintosh was developing a highly personal architectural language that had some resonances of the Art Nouveau movement. Hill House in Glasgow, designed for the publisher Walter Blackie, was completed in 1903. It is a picturesque composition of roughcast walls and tiled pitched roofs punctuated by clusters of chimneys. Mackintosh designed everything from the garden to the light fittings and much of the furniture. The decorative elements have been stripped back and made more abstract. This treatment is taken through to the interiors where the timber panelling is ornamented with inlaid patterns. While the

Above Hill House by Charles Rennie Mackintosh takes its inspiration from nature and Scottish vernacular style. The asymmetrical house appears strong and fortress-like and was considered plain when received by the public in 1903.

inspiration is certainly from nature, the application is geometrical – nature is ordered through the hand of the architect.

At about the same time in Brussels, Josef Hoffmann rejected the organic flourishes of Art Nouveau in favour of a much more pared-down architecture. His Palais Stoclet was begun in 1905 and, like Hill House, is a formal massing composition where elements of the building are balanced against each other, not in a classical, symmetrical manner, but in a more abstract sense. The interiors are glorious collages of textures, materials and forms. The dining room features a glassy mosaic by Gustav Klimt depicting stylized trees. The exterior is more enigmatic, a cubist collage topped by a curious tower adorned with statues. It perhaps represents a world in transition, rejecting the traditions of the nineteenth century but still searching for an appropriate form of expression.

Some of the most personal and idiosyncratic designs in this early period emanated from Barcelona in the work of Antonio Gaudí. In 1907 he completed two 'houses' (actually apartment blocks) in the city, Casa Milà and Casa Batlló (see p. 24), two pieces of fantasy standing on opposite street corners. Almost anatomical in reference, their sinewy organic forms are unlike anything that had come before. This quirky plastic language is taken from the façade and into the public courtyard and staircase within. Even the roofs, with their twisted chimneys, are a surreal dreamscape overlooking the logical grid of the new city. This expressionistic outburst makes Gaudí almost impossible to place within history. His style is a one-off, brilliant and yet flawed; it could not be adopted by a society looking for mass housing solutions and simple construction.

The rise of the Modern Movement

A reaction against this kind of decorative approach began to occur before the First World War, as some architects looked for a style that was more rational, simple and clean. They wanted their architecture to express the feeling of a new age. In 1910 Adolf Loos built his Steiner House in Vienna, an undecorated, simple block with deeply recessed, plain-glass windows. His famous essay of 1908, *Ornament is Crime*, was later taken up as a manifesto for the new order. His work remains to this day exemplary of a pared-down, classical architecture, sombre but nonetheless inventive. His insistence on removing

Above Josef Hoffmann's Palais Stoclet is a grand, formal residence built for a Belgian industrialist and his family. The exterior is clad in white marble slabs and a curiously monumental tower is decorated with heroic statues. Palais Stoclet can be seen as a last romantic flourish before Modernism swept such decorative motifs aside.

overtly lyrical and artful decoration was one of the first signs that a different sensibility was beginning to take hold.

The First World War changed everything, creating a bloody pause in the cultural progress of Europe and demanding new political and social regimes. To some the war represented the end of one era and the beginning of a new one. Many thinkers began to reject their past and started to consider how we might live in a new world. This utopian idealism led to some of the strongest architecture of the century.

Le Corbusier
Probably the most important architectural thinker of this period was Charles Edouard Jeanneret, known as Le Corbusier. Born in Switzerland, he trained in Paris and Berlin. His early buildings display a knowing but restrained understanding of Classical architecture, which is seen in the house at La Chaux-de-Fonds that he built for his parents in 1914. At the same time he also developed his famous Domino concrete frame, an elegant, logical, structural solution to the technical problems of erecting buildings. The frame could be put up in three weeks and the walls were then infilled with lightweight blockwork after which the outsides were rendered in smooth white. This direct link between the form of construction and the aesthetic of the building was not new. It can be seen in more primitive building forms, such as the fifteenth-century timber-framed houses at Lavenham (see p.17). What was radical in Le Corbusier's work was that no additional decorative element was proposed to adorn the structure, and the interior layout was not constrained by massive structural walls. It was what it was.

Le Corbusier published his famous manifesto *Towards a New Architecture* in 1923. In this book he writes of his despair over the state of contemporary building, proclaiming that there will be 'architecture or revolution'. He urges people to look around them at the modern world and to recognize the 'new spirit' of the age. He exults in the progressive designs of motorcars, aeroplanes and factories and invites the reader to admire their simple geometric forms, radically suggesting that a house should be 'a machine for living in'. Much of what he says still resonates today: he calls on us to empty out the contents of our homes so that we can be freed from unnecessary clutter.

Above Taken from his book, Towards a New Architecture, *this sketch by Le Corbusier shows an idea for mass-produced workers' housing made from concrete and set into simple landscaped gardens.*
Opposite Antonio Gaudí's *Casa Batlló was completed in 1907 in the new quarter of Barcelona, Spain, and contains a series of apartments within a bizarre, organic façade. The roof has dragon-like scales and concrete balconies have the appearance of bones.*

In many ways this idea is exemplified in the Maison La Roche, the house Le Corbusier completed in 1923. In fact it is two houses, one built for a collector of Cubist art and another for Le Corbusier's sister-in-law. The building is conceived of as two interlocking blocks on an L-shaped plan, creating an end to the street on which it is sited. The aesthetics of the building are uncompromisingly modern. Horizontal metal windows arranged in a run or featured as abstract, punched squares punctuate the white walls. The building appears to be more of an object sitting in space than a house set into a streetscape. The volumes within are skilfully manipulated: devoid of decorative elements the spaces are ingeniously lit from the side and above and each surface is chosen to form an abstract composition of colour. This abstraction owed much to the art of the Cubists which the architect admired and studied; he was a painter himself and devoted half of his day to his canvases.

Le Corbusier's design for the Villa Savoye has an iconic status within the history of architecture. Built in 1929 and sited in Poissy outside Paris, this is the ultimate 'object' house, a stark white box hovering in a green field. The villa has all the characteristics of a

Above Sitting alone within a green field outside Paris, the Villa Savoye remains one of the twentieth century's most memorable buildings. Its Functionalist aesthetic boldly embodies Le Corbusier's 'five points of New Architecture': the use of piloti, the roof garden, the free plan, the free façade and the ribbon window. *Left* Le Corbusier's industrial aesthetic can still be seen in his Villa Sarabhai of 1955, but here he uses a collage of earthy materials and bright colours.

Modernist building. It sits on slender columns (called piloti) which are spaced around the turning circle of a car. The circulation sequence includes both staircases and ramps, and there is a sculptural roof terrace. While the exterior is predominantly white, the interior is clad in tiles and the surfaces are painted delicate shades of blue and pink.

In The Netherlands, too, there were protagonists of the Modern Movement. The architect Gerrit Rietveld completed a most unconventional house for Truus Shröder in Utrecht in 1924. The site was the small, unassuming end of a terrace; the client a determined, intellectual woman who wanted to create an experimental home in which to bring up her children. The result is a delightful three-dimensional jigsaw puzzle. From the outside the house looks like a box with a series of layers and planes spaced in front − the façade is literally a composition of elements. A balcony at first-floor level is a cantilevered slab of concrete which has two curved horizontal railings connecting back to a terrace partly concealed behind a floating plane. There are also a variety of windows which create a strong sense of void within the solid construction. Within, the plan is ingenious: sliding walls can be used to open and close off zones depending on how the house is being occupied. This sense of flexibility was certainly very forward-looking and remains an inspiring piece of modern design.

New technology and the rational

It has often been said that war forces technology to advance and this was certainly true of the First World War. New developments in the design of aircraft saw the use of lightweight materials and aerodynamic forms. Temporary shelters and aircraft hangars were prefabricated using the latest production-line technology. In the light of the atrocities of the war and the inevitable economic hardship the idea of simple, modern design seemed, at least to some, to suggest a future free from the baggage of the past and one that celebrated the honesty of these new forms. We have already seen how the Modernists rejected history in a bid to wipe the slate clean. For many the expression of a new order was to be achieved by seeing the world as a potentially purer and more rational place.

The architectural manifestation of this belief was to become known as Functionalism, and the German architect Ludwig Mies van der Rohe was its most

Above Looking like a Mondrian painting executed in three dimensions, the compositional sophistication of the Schröder House in Utrecht by Gerrit Rietveld is a remarkable example of the new post-war architecture.

famous proponent. Although he had been classically trained, in the 1920s Mies van der Rohe's designs became increasingly abstract and his ideas more and more pared down. In 1928 he finished the Krefeld House, an elegant brick box punctured by large expanses of glass. While not a house as such, his famous 'Barcelona Pavilion', which was built for the 1929 World Exposition in Spain, alludes to a new way of domestic living. It has flowing, open-plan spaces, walls that are vast planes of marble and stone and scant, carefully placed furniture. While not quite minimal, his clean lines and geometric expression are tightly controlled and his influence on house design is still felt to this day.

Another example of such housing can be seen in the German town of Dessau, home of the influential Bauhaus between 1925 and 1933. Here, Walter Gropius, director of this revolutionary design school, constructed a new building of glass and concrete that incorporated the very latest principles of Functionalism. Gropius also designed homes nearby for the professors of the school. These were white, box-like compositions on the outside, but contained delightful collages of coloured planes within. One of the houses, for the artist Paul Klee,

Above The pared-down dining room of the Feininger House in Dessau reflects the spirit of the Bauhaus. The colour scheme, however, is a carefully chosen palette of different tones and shades intended to make each room an architectural whole. *Left* The table and chairs were designed in 1925 by Marcel Breuer, head of the Bauhaus furniture workshop. They remain iconic and are still seen as quintessentially modern pieces.

even has gold leaf around the door frames on the ground floor. This surprising use of colour reminds us that the Modernist architects were not necessarily 'minimalist' and enjoyed the richness and experience that colour offers.

Soft Modernism Another expression of this new form displayed a much more organic sensibility. This was not the fantasy of Art Nouveau or Antonio Gaudí, but a more studied, sensuous architecture. The designs of Finnish architect Alvar Aalto were revolutionary and beautiful, combining natural forms with modern, machine-age lines. Today he is remembered as a humanist for his very particular understanding of the way people like to live. His Villa Mairea, built in Finland and completed in 1939, has an elegant L-shaped plan which opens out on to a series of courtyards and a kidney-shaped swimming pool. Aalto's sensual enjoyment of how light works against natural surfaces is key to his architectural language and the materials he used were very important to him. Some of the external walls are clad in timber, reflecting the woodland setting, and this theme continues inside, achieving an almost rustic quality in places that harks back to the

simple rural hut. This impression is reinforced by the stone-clad fireplace and open-plan spaces. The interior is also punctuated by columns and wooden poles in a deliberate reference to the Finnish forest, completing the synthesis between the natural world and the manmade environment.

Rebuilding and rebranding By the end of the Second World War much of Europe had been devastated. Many soldiers returned home to find that they had nowhere to live. Much of this was due to bomb damage, but in many cities there were also swathes of slums, mainly of the nineteenth century, which had been condemned. There was an acute housing shortage and funds were channelled into rebuilding programmes.

A British report of 1945 suggested that four million homes would be required in the next ten years. The government built temporary houses, laid out in military rows, and called them 'homes for heroes', though in reality they were poorly constructed affairs made of steel and asbestos. It is worth noting that during this period materials were rationed, if available at all, so architects had little freedom of expression. The whole of Europe

Above The Villa Mairea, Noormakku, Finland, was built by Alvar Aalto as a weekend retreat for a wealthy couple. The clean lines of this elegant Modernist home are balanced by sensuous curves and timber-clad walls. Inside the house is a collage of natural materials whose rustic overtones are tempered by a sense of scale and complexity.

became a massive construction site, repairing and rebuilding the infrastructure, restoring historic buildings and demolishing damaged and old housing to replace it with new. It was also generally accepted that the State would take a role in procuring the accommodation required for the displaced and growing population. The new architecture took its cue from the pre-war period relating to the 'International Style' (see p.35). Cities such as Hanover in Germany, Coventry in Great Britain and Rotterdam in Holland all had to face substantial reconstruction. It is worth noting that much of the interesting and cutting-edge development in housing was happening a long way off in countries less affected by the war such as South America, Japan and Hong Kong. In America the development of the curtain wall, a glass façade that could be hung from steel or concrete frames, became the new motif favoured for residential and office buildings alike.

The 1940s saw the production of 'Utility' furniture which professed to be good, simple and useful design. While it fulfilled its function it was hardly the fruit of a brave new world. In 1949, however, the Ideal Home Exhibition in London included a display entitled the 'Pavilion of Beautiful

Above *After the Second World War the housing shortage throughout Europe was addressed by providing simple prefabricated homes for returning soldiers and their families. These pictures illustrate the instant domesticity that could be achieved using cost-efficient system building.*

Things' which began to look forward to a world of luxury and choice. The Festival of Britain provided an important focus for design in 1951. It was conceived of as a political tool to kickstart interest in construction and production as well as to popularize a government in trouble. The impact of the Festival is still debated, but suffice to say that it remains a turning-point in British design and even though it was dismantled by the incoming government, its ripples were felt nationally. In terms of housing, a new estate was built in the borough of Poplar in London which was seen as a blueprint for a 'Live Architecture' exhibition linked to the Festival. The scheme was conceived as an opportunity to present a cross-section of different kinds of urban development for Poplar. It was made up of terraced housing and low flat blocks, which architect Frederick Gibberd stated were intended to form pleasant spaces on a human scale.

But while architects and designers began to take up the modernist mantle again, the general public was less inclined to embrace their utopian vision. There was a feeling that people wanted to ally themselves with their history and did not wish to live in brave experiments.

A new world While Europe was looking at advertisements that proclaimed 'Lucky is the mother whose table is Formica-topped', the United States was thriving and the wealthy, young middle classes wanted to live in modern homes. A number of influential thinkers and architects had emigrated to the United States in the late 1930s, fearing the outbreak of war, among them Mies van der Rohe and Walter Gropius. These European Modernists were to have an important impact on post-war American architecture. Mies van der Rohe's seminal Farnsworth House of 1946, in Plano, Illinois, was really a glass pavilion, suggesting a generic but elegant solution to the problem of the individual house. The building, designed as a weekend retreat, was conceived as an essay in minimalism. It remains a seductive icon of a more innocent world. The client, Edith Farnsworth, professed to be horrified by the outcome, at the time saying it was like an X-ray.

Five years later architect Philip Johnson proposed his own version of the glass pavilion in New Canaan, Connecticut (see p.32). His house is certainly influenced by Mies van der Rohe, but it sits firmly bedded on the ground. Both homes enjoy the luxury of isolation; they are set in generous grounds

Above Viewed through the trees, Mies van der Rohe's Farnsworth House of 1946 appears as an ethereal glass box floating beneath a steel frame. It remains a powerful and seductive vision for a modern house and has been much copied, despite the fact that the client was always uneasy about the design.

giving a rarefied sense of escapism and connection with nature. It seemed as though this revolution of transparency was here to stay.

A more personal version of the steel-and-glass home was proposed by Charles and Ray Eames in their Santa Monica house of 1949. This was constructed from standard components rather than specially made parts and had a machine-made aesthetic, which was tempered by the use of colour and its natural setting. The couple were interested in redefining ideas of domesticity and did not want to eradicate all traces of inhabitation. They travelled widely and collected objects and souvenirs which they displayed without embarrassment. They mixed the everyday with the exotic, creating an interior that was a true reflection of their personalities. The double-height space inside is characterized by the full-height window wall on one side and mirrored by a timber wall opposite. The kitchen is situated beneath the balcony, which also acts as a landing; the soffit is a crinkly metal profile held up by fine exposed metal trusses. Looking at the house today it still has a relevant industrial aesthetic but it is not cold and alienating – and even though built over half a century ago, still appears fresh and contemporary.

Australia was also emerging as a hotbed of contemporary design. One significant example can be identified as the house completed in Sydney by the young architect Harry Seidler in 1948 (see p.34). The architect, who had been born in Vienna and trained in America, had emigrated to Australia and the house was built for his family. The result is a white box that perches on a rough stone garden wall and is held up by slender steel columns. It has an almost nautical feel with its white, cantilevered, slatted sunshades and a colourful mural painted on the flank wall of the open raised courtyard. This building competed directly with the architecture of Europe and America, demonstrating that Australia, although far away from Europe, was exploring the same issues and developing its own regional identity.

Global modernity

By the 1950s Modernism was a global phenomenon and much housing was universally constructed from concrete and glass. This architectural language, which had once been considered avant garde, had been absorbed into that of the everyday. Tower blocks of flats were increasingly common. Originally conceived of by Le Corbusier as a way of achieving a 'garden city' by

Above Maverick American architect Philip Johnson designed his version of a glass house in New Canaan, Connecticut, in 1949. Illuminated at night, the house appears to have no walls at all and blends into its natural setting.

freeing up the land around to make parks, they were squeezed into any number of urban sites or marooned in empty space. Le Corbusier built his own powerful example, the Unité d'Habitation in Marseilles, France, which was completed in 1953. The building is a long slab which is 12 storeys high and made from concrete. Each apartment is expressed on the front by a recessed balcony. The whole building is held up off the ground on pillars with only the lift and stairtower landing at ground-level. The rooftop – housing a gym and a crèche – is a collection of sculptural objects and was conceived as a kind of garden. These apartments were carefully designed with the needs of people and their families in mind. The balconies were seen as an 'outdoor' room and there are generous double-height spaces inside each home as well as communal areas in corridors and circulation spaces. Outside the tower is surrounded by a park.

This model was subsequently adopted by many as the way forward, often to disastrous effect. While it gave the illusion of being universal and ideological, it was in fact designed for the site and the Mediterranean climate, where the sun casts great shadows across the building and rain does not easily

stain the concrete. Later generations rejected the idea that architecture and housing could be understood as absolute solutions, and that there should be more attention paid to the location, climate and end user. Le Corbusier's work in India, where he designed the city of Chandigarh north of New Delhi, was on a different scale again. Whole neighbourhoods of housing were made of concrete, laid around public squares and precincts. Much of his work remains and – though the concrete is rough and the open spaces scrubby – its visual impact cannot be underestimated. But his house of 1955 for the Sarabhai family in Ahmedabad is perhaps more satisfactory (see p.26). Here Le Corbusier developed a spacious home built from concrete with eight half-barrel vaulted ceilings. The roof is covered in grass creating a thermal mass that keeps the house cool in summer and acts as a quilt in winter. The house sits around a pool and there is a delightful sculptural concrete slide which drops from the roof into the pool.

The global revolution of the 1950s had been fuelled by economic growth and a new-found prosperity. The sense of expanding consumer choice was reinforced by new designs of objects for the

Above Known as 'Case Study House 8', the home built by Charles and Ray Eames in Santa Monica, California, is a lightweight, steel-framed construction clad in corrugated metal and glass. The playful use of coloured textiles and objets trouvés to furnish the interior suggests a more approachable methodology than that of other Modernists.

home; the age of product design had arrived. This was made possible by new mass-production technologies such as vacuum injection-moulding and increasingly sophisticated mechanization. The age of the 'lifestyle' had dawned.

The good, the bad and the ugly

At the beginning of the 1960s the modernist house seemed to be in the ascendant. Younger architects inspired by the work of Le Corbusier were given the opportunity to build. Alison and Peter Smithson proposed an innovative new workers' housing scheme for Golden Lane in London (1952). The slab blocks of flats were to have had open deck access, which were seen as streets in the sky, and were of an architectural style that was labelled 'New Brutalism'. This term was coined by the critics of the day as a heroic and powerful epithet, though it now has far more pejorative overtones. There remained the idealized notion that, as in the terraced slums the blocks were to replace, there would be a sense of neighbourhood and the chance encounters one had on the street would still happen up in the air.

While this project remained on paper many others in the Brutalist genre were built, despite the fact that concrete architecture – and the social engineering it embodied – was heavily criticized by the public. A backlash began, the repercussions of which we still feel today. Many complained that their mass-produced homes were flimsy and inadequate. The tower blocks did not sit in the beautifully managed parks envisioned by Le Corbusier. While in the best examples of this new way of living his ideals remained intact, the avarice of many developers and councils resulted in hordes of substandard, badly designed, socially naive homes. There were some successful buildings of this period, however, surviving examples of which are Roehampton Estate in London by LCC Architects; and Gallaratese 11 in Milan by Aldo Rossi. It is said that a major turning-point in modern social history was the blowing up in 1975 of Minoru Yamasaki's Pruitt-Igoe housing project in St Louis, Missouri, United States. This great monolithic development had only been built for about 20 years but was reviled by its occupants who found it a bleak, unfriendly place to live. (The architect went on to design the World Trade Centre.) This act of demolition signified the end of this era of architecture and people began to look elsewhere for inspiration.

Above The Rose Seidler House in Sydney (1948) was the first building completed by Harry Seidler, an architect at the vanguard of modern Australian design. This Modernist concrete box is held up on skinny steel columns and appears almost on the verge of being launched into the sea.

A change in the air Modernist architecture, inspired by rational uniformity, had become so widespread that it became known as the 'International Style', a term first coined in the 1930s. It began to seem as if buildings looked the same wherever you went. One reaction was to look back at ideas of regional difference, perhaps because people resented the break with history that this kind of architecture demanded. One of the first examples of this approach is a house built in 1964 by Robert Venturi for his mother in Philadelphia, United States (see p.36). It has even been hailed as the first 'Post-Modern' home, as the architecture was deliberately playful and irreverent in the way it stylized the building elements and made reference to historical motifs. The house is solid and box-like with a pitched roof but, instead of meeting, the gables of the roof split to leave a gap. The architecture itself is not obviously radical, but this mixture of 'quotations' was something quite new and expressed a desire to create a richer and more decorative modern idiom.

Nearby in the Hamptons on Long Island, a cluster of elegant and glamorous seaside homes was built for weekenders from New York. Among them is an important house by the young Charles Gwathmey, which he also designed for his mother in 1963 (see p.36). From the outside it is a collection of monolithic forms, featuring at roof-level a massive picture window that seems to scoop the view from the sea into the interior. While this house still makes a strong formal statement, there are signs that some of the ideas are derived from personal intuition rather than a rigorous intellectual framework. His love of the curve is clearly a Modernist device which he plays with in a sculptural, almost free-form way.

During the 1970s there was much discussion of new Post-Modern ideas. The movement can be seen broadly as a reaction to the perceived linear thinking of Modernism; it suggested that you could borrow from history and collage together ideas and styles. There was a sense in which anything went, and the more radical the better. The house was an excellent vehicle for the advancement of this new architectural conceit which, by the 1980s, was reflected in the homes people built for themselves. A rather eclectic series of projects ensued, ranging from the Classical revival of Quinlan Terry to the self-contained houses of Peter Eiserman. Eiserman built a series of extremely complex homes in the United States as well as a curious housing block in

Above Minoru Yamasaki's Pruitt-Igoe housing project in St Louis, United States, was such a rigid and alien environment and was so different to the surrounding city that it became an island ghetto. The vision had been to create a utopia but the reality was distopia.

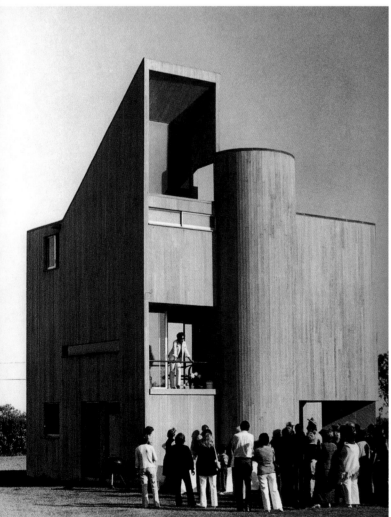

Berlin, completed in 1987. Here we see how the issues of geometry and balance, so prized by architects of earlier generations, are questioned: façades are slanted, windows are layered and a series of visual games often leaves the onlooker puzzled.

Yet another twist in the tail may be traced to 1979, when the architect Frank Gehry remodelled his own, rather ordinary, clapboard house in Santa Monica, California, into a sculptural extravaganza. He made a metal frame from steel poles and mesh to create a series of boxes and balconies on the outside. Inside it looks as though another building or construction has collided with it. It was not long before this, too, was labelled as a new movement – 'Deconstruction'.

A new generation The single most important factor that changed the way people designed and built houses at the beginning of the twentieth century was the development of concrete, glass and steel. While concrete had been discovered by the Romans, it was the use of pre-stressed steel embedded within concrete that gave it much more strength and flexibility. This technology remains the most generic and global form of mass

Above Marking a radical departure from stark, white Modernism, Robert Venturi's house for his mother showed a more playful approach to architecture, mixing traditional motifs with quirky composition.
Left American architect Charles Gwathmey designed a house on the beach for his parents in Long Island, New York, which is an expressive collection of timber-clad primary forms.

construction though building itself is still generally a messy business. What has changed radically at the beginning of the twenty-first century is the way in which people design. The introduction of the computer as a design tool has meant that new, more complicated forms can be drawn and subsequently built. In some cases the information that made the computer model in the design office is fed directly to the factory and used to manufacture individual components. This means even more flexibility than before. The old adage that mass production would mean cheap but well-designed homes for all has been challenged in the sense that the tools developed for mass production can now be subverted to create special, one-off designs.

Other global issues are changing the way we live, among them the 'green' agenda. Since the 1973 oil crisis there has been growing concern over our use of natural resources. House building not only consumes huge amounts of building materials but there are massive ongoing costs as water, electricity, oil or gas all have to be supplied to maintain the modern home. These are often taken for granted but there is now pressure to make homes that recycle building materials and take less energy to

run. Environmentally aware architecture is not characterized by a particular style, but more by its general approach. For example, much of the world expects to have air-conditioned homes: a building may be insulated in all sorts of ways to stop it losing or gaining heat. Is it possible to design spaces that are naturally ventilated? Glass itself can be treated to allow views in and out but to prevent heat transfer, thus saving on fuel to heat or cool a space. The use of solar panels can greatly assist the reduction of energy consumption in the home.

A new wave of designers, aware of such issues and able to exploit computer technology to solve them, are now at the vanguard of 'home making'. One of the most influential is the Dutch architect Rem Koolhaas. Over the past 15 years he has designed a number of mass housing projects as well as individual homes. His Maison à Bordeaux built in 1988 in Floriac, France, is a challenging structural composition (see p. 38). The top floor looks like a great solid beam floating over a glass box. At the centre of the house is an ingenious moving platform that works as a lift. The owner is wheelchair-bound and the design of the house is sensitive to his needs, providing uninterrupted floor space and great views.

Above The remodelling of his Santa Monica house in 1979 allowed architect Frank Gehry to explore a new aesthetic now referred to as 'Deconstruction'. His suburban house was wrapped and pierced by a collection of everyday materials transforming it into a unique and experimental home.

Another experimental house that explores new forms is the Möbius House built by UN Studio and designed by architects Van Berkel and Boss in Het Gool, The Netherlands. Here the overall concept is linked to the way the circulation moves around in a loop; the space is literally twisted. Built from glass and concrete the house appears to be a conglomeration of parts. It is a long way from a traditional house, with the emphasis on complex spatial relationships rather than four square 'rooms'.

This brief survey has pointed out a number of milestones in the development of the home. As we look at the present it is more difficult to pinpoint those houses that may be representative of our age; with the explosion of digital technology and an image-making culture there are new things to look at every day. As far as the home is concerned this must be a good thing. It seems to suggest that the concept of the house is always in flux, and there will always be another architect and client willing to journey into the unknown, to sculpt and mould a house to their own specific needs. While the results may not directly affect the majority, history has shown that design filters down. Something new yesterday becomes commonplace today.

Opposite above At the
Maison à Bordeaux by
Rem Koolhaas traditional
structural logic is defied as
the transparency of the
ground floor reveals all the
secrets within. There is a
tension between the rough
texture of the concrete and
the minimal glass detailing.
Opposite below The Möbius
House, built in 1998 by
UN Studio, is a complex
composition of concrete and
glass which blurs the
boundary between inside
and outside. Above The
stark living and dining area
within the Möbius House
defies accepted notions
of cosy domesticity.

2. House and Home

House and Home
Identity and Self-expression

In 1939, in *The Book of the Modern House*, its editor Patrick Abercrombie attempted a sample survey of modern domestic architecture and interiors. Within its pages we see an eclectic mix of classical, vernacular and modern design. Although Abercrombie appeared keen to advocate progress he nevertheless suggested that the austere interiors presented by the Modernists would, in the long run, be pushed aside for cosier, more familiar styles. It is as though he were conceding that the burden of history cannot be forgotten, and that modernity was akin to fashion: once the fad had passed we would go back to a more traditional way of life. This, of course, was all about to change with the advent of war. However it seems that today the wheel has now come full circle and the pressure to fill our homes with 'stuff' has never been greater.

So what is it that people are looking for when they replace their modern windows with Tudor leaded lights, their kitchen cupboards with antique pine doors and their smooth concrete façades with rusticated stone? (It should be stressed that this is largely a Western phenomenon: in the new Asian tiger economies people are far less interested in hanging on to their old lives and view a modern apartment block filled with modern things as a sign

of progress.) It is a question of identity and nostalgia. For many, an object's authenticity – its inherent emotional and functional value – is important. The home can be seen as embodying both.

Western culture remains in a state of transition; there is a love of the past but a desire for the future. The present itself is ever more elusive and invisible. Many of the gadgets in our homes operate without us being able to witness the way they work. They are not machines with visible moving parts; they are abstract technology. There is then a new problem of aesthetics: what do these things look like? There is no right way for a computer or dishwasher to look. As technology gets smaller, its 'packaging' needs redesigning. What is more, market forces inevitably dictate that people should keep buying and replacing redundant tools. Who wants a ten-year-old mobile phone? Yet many of us will value a 50-year-old typewriter, or an eighteenth-century cottage. In the well-publicized 'makeover' programmes on television, rooms become fantasy stage-sets. Why

not have a bedroom like a battleship or a dining room that looks baronial? We can do as we wish.

A roof above our heads

Today many do not see living in a house as a luxury, but as something taken for granted. We expect to have the utilities that modern living affords: electricity, hot and cold water, and protection from the elements. This is still not the case in many parts of the world, and indeed it has only been so in the West in the last 50 years, since we have attempted to define and regulate a 'standard of living'. The new-build house is designed to meet the needs of today's lifestyles and many have built-in flexibility to allow for different patterns of living. It is not always easy, however, to design a dwelling that is both flexible and which has a sense of permanence. For the projects in this book, architects and their clients have engaged in a searching enquiry into the nature of the modern house, how it is expressed and how it engages the world around it.

Opposite This inhabited interior reflects the interests and collections of the owner whose belongings remain unashamedly on display. *Above* In contrast, this apartment designed by Claudio Silvestrin is a homage to minimalist living. All potential clutter, including books, is housed in an almost invisible wall storage system.

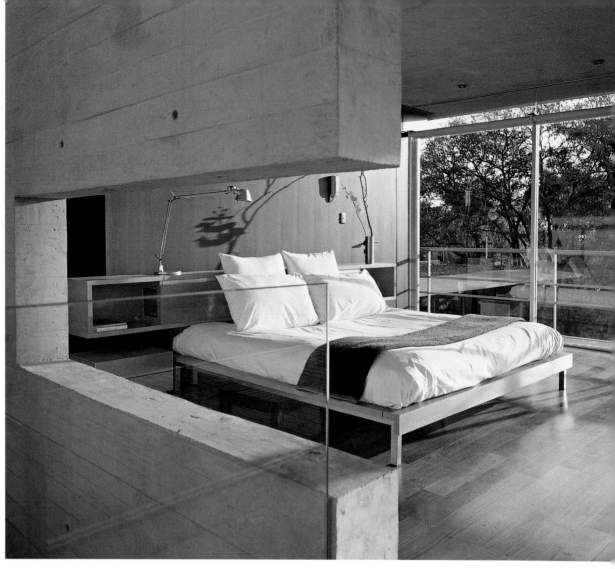

Above left The interior of this apartment is kept as open as possible by using a series of floating timber screens dividing off the dining from the living area and the bathroom from the bedroom. The result is both formal and yet delightful.

Above right A narrow slot cut into an internal wall lets in light from the stairwell, but also maintains a degree of privacy in this bedroom.

Open house One of the most crucial differences between the modern home and the traditional one is the way in which space is divided up. The concept of having to create rooms to satisfy certain social mores – using the front room only on special occasions, for example – is almost dead. Space is one of the greatest luxuries of our time, especially in the city, and it follows that there should be no wasted space in the modern home. There are exceptions, however; when looking at the homes of the very rich, many of whom have staff, a large number of rooms is not only desirable, but is a necessity that must be accommodated in the design.

Very different spatial relationships and configurations are now possible, giving us far greater freedom to explore and express exactly how we want to live. In the late twentieth century the notion of open-plan living, or 'loft living', became fashionable. The original loft-livers were artists who used to sleep in their studios. They often formed communities in areas that were neglected and so had cheap property available to rent or even squat. The meat market in New York was home to many

fashionable artists who inhabited disused warehouses. Today loft living is freely used to describe a lifestyle in which a number of activities can take place in the same room: cooking, eating, sleeping, and so on. The only space that remains sacred is the bathroom; besides the many practical reasons why bathrooms and eating do not mix, there is also a taboo which is unlikely to be displaced.

External boundaries, marking the zone between private and public, are also important. In large, detached houses the boundary may be a wall or hedge, and a gateway is the only clue to what lies behind. In more densely inhabited areas the door to the house can be just off the street and in this situation net curtains appear at windows, designer handles on doors. Each of these are messages communicating something about those who live within. Because we value the fact that our homes have an identity, that they create a sense of place and wellbeing, we like customizing them in this way. This is especially true in mass housing when the basic unit is repetitive but can be easily subverted by a new front door or a coat of exterior paint.

Everyday and the special Most people have some kind of routine, the substance of the everyday: getting up in the morning, going to work, coming home. These activities are generally considered mundane and unremarkable. By contrast there are other activities that are considered special, often because they involve ritual: people staying the night, hosting a wedding party, Sunday lunch… In these cases the routine of everyday life is thrown off and a different set of priorities is undertaken. Both conditions are made possible within the home.

For us to go about our daily lives there has to be a regime of order in the home. Things have their places and should be accessed with minimum fuss. When we are talking about the setting for an event, then the requirements are different. It may mean rearranging the furniture of a room, getting out different china or opening up a sliding door to make two spaces into one. Such considerations form only one aspect of designing an interior, but it is an important one as it represents the psychological space of the home. The reality of everyday life can be transformed by the setting in which it occurs.

There is currently a revival of interest in ideas about 'the everyday' which informs the work of some new designers. The Marshall House in Suffolk, by Dow Jones Architects (see p.102), is an excellent example. This new building uses local materials, mostly in a traditional way, but there are also knowing details such as the different window sizes, the way in which the timber inside wraps on to the ceiling and even the scale of the house in the landscape. The overall form of the building suggests that it might always have been there, and in that sense it is in the family of local buildings. The subtle additions to the traditional diagram show how it has become a building of the twentieth century.

Place of memory The homes we live in are filled with our memories. These may take many forms. Today we attribute great importance to objects that may have no intrinsic worth but have a personal history. (Ironically in the present context, people who have lost their homes in a flood or fire sometimes declare that their most tragic loss is not the house itself but the contents: photographs of

Above The living room of the Marshall House by Dow Jones Architects has been designed using the traditional materials of brick, timber and plaster to create a simple yet cleverly contemporary space which is ready to be inhabited by the new owners.

Above Raised up on piloti, the rear façade of the F2 House in Mexico by Miguel Adria, Isaac Broid and Michael Rojkind, is a graphic composition of slots and frameless windows. During the day the building is a solid object in the landscape, while at night it appears more transparent – a box floating within a box.

family, some treasured jewellery or souvenirs of a distant past.) It is worth noting that this is a relatively new concept. In the eighteenth century people owned things because they were useful, valuable or beautiful. The concept of bric-a-brac simply did not exist.

But the structure of the home itself may carry important memories. Although it seems that we are always being encouraged to redecorate and update our homes, there is something very reassuring about materials that have weathered over time: timber floorboards that have been worn down, a brass handrail that is particularly shiny in parts, peeling paint revealing more layers beneath. This sense of ageing carries with it the price of becoming old, the possibility that the lines, scratches and wrinkles may be unattractive – there is a fine line between a surface that has been touched and worn in a pleasing way and one that looks dirty, neglected and damaged. It is one of the biggest criticisms of modern architecture that the 'white box' can be so daunting as to be almost unliveable in. One dirty mark and the whole place feels spoiled and dilapidated. People often have an almost paranoid fear that architects only endorse this kind of minimalism and that they will be forced to throw away all their possessions. For a very few this is a beautiful way of life but for most of us it is the synthesis of place-making, of uniting the way we aspire to live and the way we have to live, that is the key to the inspiring examples of the New Home.

The language of architecture The distinction between what is classified as simply a building and what constitutes architecture is a difficult call. While it is often a personal judgement, it could be said that architecture is created when the whole experience is more than the sum of the parts. When people talk about building design they often mention the language of architecture, referring to the way in which a string of elements makes up a meaningful whole. In considering architecture, and in this case domestic architecture, it is important to pay attention to the nature of the individual elements and to understand their significance in relation to each other and to an entire building.

The popular image of the house is often a childlike diagram of a square box, punctuated by four square windows, with a front door and a pitched roof. It is a kind of paradigm for the perfect house, a neat self-contained home which is symmetrical and unchallenging. Indeed, many such homes have been built across Europe and the United States but most are not, sadly, examples of architectural harmony. The diagram does not take into account the complex relationships whereby these units come together to form towns and cities. Yet it remains culturally embedded and serves as a starting-point when reviewing the nature and aspiration of the individual house.

One interesting example of a house that uses this image but radically questions it is the Rudin House in Leymen, France, designed by Herzog and de Meuron. From a distance it may look familiar, with its square windows, pitched roof and central chimney, but on closer inspection the house is seen to be made entirely of concrete and sitting on a floating concrete plinth. The windows are bigger than expected and the frames are made of natural timber which somewhat softens the impact of the raw concrete finishes. At night, ground-level lights reflect upwards on to the plinth creating the rather disconcerting impression that the building is floating.

Many of the case studies later in this book challenge the preconceptions people may have about houses. They are often built around a concrete or steel frame so do not have conventional walls. The use of glass is notable; windows do not have to be set in standard frames, they can be walls made of glass held in invisible metal angles. Roofs can be almost flat or manifest themselves as more playful compositions, depending on the massing and volume of the building. Whatever form it might take, it can be said that the individual expression of the modern home reflects to a large extent the changing circumstances of the present day.

Inside out By looking at the outside of a house it is possible to glean clues as to the organization of the interior. The theory of functionalism proposes that there should be a one-to-one correlation between domestic requirements, internal layout and

external expression. Therefore a fireplace is reflected in a chimney and a porch signifies the front door; the kitchen window may be a long horizontal slot while the bathroom has a small square window of opaque glass. It was precisely this simple equation that so appealed to the Modernist designers; it represented a truth to function and form, and it was an obvious tactic to expel the surface decoration of earlier historical periods. The relationship between the inside and outside of a house is vital when designing a new home: the issue is not just functional but is also stylistic. From the outside the house is a statement; it cannot help revealing something about those who built it and those who inhabit it.

Many people enjoy having a garden and even in the densest urban sites there may be a flourishing roof terrace or balcony. This need to bring the countryside into our homes is very common and is part of the dialogue between things that are manmade and things that are natural. In Japan people often live in tiny, minimalist apartments that allow no space for clutter. They almost always contain a single plant, however, placed in a prominent position as a symbol of nature. This connection to the seasons and the nurturing required by plants adds another dimension to the homes we live in.

Other signals of inhabitation are found in the things around the house; a shed, a swing, a letter box

Above In designing the Rudin House, architects Herzog and de Meuron sought to embrace a traditional form, but at the same time to transform it by building the whole structure out of concrete. The result is both charming and austere.

on the gate, a swimming pool and, of course, a car. All of these accoutrements are choices that people have made and as such reflect personal tastes and aspirations. The garage is a relatively new problem for house designers, who have produced a myriad of solutions, either incorporating it into the fabric of the building or making a separate structure. Often garages are ill-considered and unsatisfactory, treated as necessary but unwanted add-ons.

The threshold, the point between outside and inside, may be a simple front step or a whole procession of events, from a gate to a porch and into the hallway. These formal entrances are different to the more secretive back doorways, often not visible from the street, which by their nature are low key. In some cases the site will dictate the way into the house while in others, particularly when the house stands alone, it forms part of the conceit of the design.

Although balconies or decks may be accessible from the entrance they are often considered to be 'outside' rooms which can be used seasonally. One extreme example of this is Shigeru Ban's Curtain House in Tokyo. The house is designed as a frame with parking at street-level and two further floors of accommodation above. Glass doors across the two open sides can be completely folded back in a reverse of the normal relationship between public and private as the home opens up to look over the street. Huge white curtains can be drawn in front to create a soft fabric enclosure. The effect is startling and yet strangely familiar, like a tent.

Composition and form

The term 'composition' implies balance and the considered placement of elements to form a whole. In the world of painting and sculpture, composition is one of the key aspects to think about when evaluating a work. It does not necessarily imply that there is a right or wrong way of doing things, but the result may be judged from the relationship between different parts. The modern house plays with the spatial opportunities afforded by compositional freedom. This may be done in a very subtle and sensitive way, especially within a historic context, or it may be wilfully gymnastic and eye-catching.

When buildings are described as vernacular it usually means that they are traditional in their material and detail; they may also relate to a particular method of building that is historically rooted in the area. In rural areas, the vernacular architecture tends to consist of farmhouse and barn,

Left By night the formal composition of the House and Studio by Mecanoo Architects is thrown into relief as the building becomes a shadow punctuated by large windows. Below left Within, the composition of robust materials is tempered by the presence of everyday cooking utensils and paraphernalia.

cottage and homestead. These traditional forms and compositions are currently being given interesting interpretations by a number of designers who are keen to relate new and old types of construction through the use of form, but not necessarily through detail. The Pool House in Wiltshire, England, by London-based AHMM Architects, makes reference to the form of a barn with its gently barrel-vaulted roof and simple punched windows, but instead of being made out of corrugated metal it is clad in cedar boards. The end elevation is glazed, allowing uninterrupted views across the fields.

In Japan the idea of designing a minimalist house is taken to extremes in the work of Tadao Ando, who creates sheer concrete façades that give nothing away to the outside world. In his Koshino House in Ashiya, Hyogo, Japan, a small slot creates

the entrance to an interior courtyard which is used as an outside room. This narrow space acts as a light trap and all the windows in the house open on to it. The composition is all about a dialogue between open and closed spaces and openings.

At the opposite end of the spectrum domestic architecture can be much more expressive and dynamic. In the House and Studio, in Rotterdam, Holland, Mecanoo Architects took a layered approach to the façades. The structure is a steel frame from which screens and balconies are hung. The large bamboo screen on the side façade is hung from a channel in which it can slide, allowing the occupiers to change the amount and quality of sunlight entering the space. In the daytime the house appears solid but at night light seeps through the screens and the large picture windows allow views

Above This white cube of a house by the Japanese architectural practice FOBA is a graphic example of how reductive the form and detail of a house can become. A large square opening to one side reveals glimpses of a sheltered courtyard and more layered series of interior spaces.

into the interior and the life of the house. While the
cubic form of the house is simple and easily
understood, the layout of the rooms inside is less
obvious as the definition between solid walls and
moveable screens is ambiguous.

A similarly elemental approach is seen in the
Nerima House in Tokyo by Itsko Hasagawa. This
building is expressed as a collection of parts. A stair,
which appears to be cut out of a sheet of metal,
connects the two concrete boxes that make up the
separate parts of the house, one for the parents and
the other for their daughter. A curved metal roof
covers both of the dwellings and out of the top
peeks a platform from which to look out at the
moon. The architect makes a play between shapes
that appear natural and those that are manmade.
The result is a highly individual expression that
reflects the living arrangements of the family.

Structure Any building has to be designed to
stand up. This basic rule seems obvious enough, but
there have been plenty of examples where it has
been overlooked. Cases of aspiration outstripping
available technology can be found in some early
twentieth-century houses which looked as though
they were made of concrete, but were in fact made
of brick and rendered over, including Le Corbusier's
famous Villa Savoye (see p. 26). After a few decades
the poorly built brickwork of some buildings began
to move and the render cracked and fell off, making
some structurally unsound.

Today much more sophisticated choices for
construction are available, which means that
structural gymnastics are possible. Mass housing
tends to use safe construction techniques that rely
on the four-square brick box to offer stability and
support. The opposite is true of the individual house,

however. Frank Lloyd Wright's masterpiece, Fallingwater, is a series of concrete terraces that appear to float over a waterfall. The cantilever tests the structural property of concrete to its limits. A more recent example is the Susuki House in Tokyo, a tiny concrete box with just enough space to park a car beneath, by German-based architects Bolles Wilson. The house uses monolithic concrete construction: it is supported by a sheer wall on one side while an expressive pair of concrete legs on the other holds up the heavy cantilever. Within is a double-height void punctured by another cantilevered box that contains the bedroom.

Materials

The way in which houses are made is expressed on the outside by the materials that are visible. In many concrete or steel-frame houses the actual structure is concealed behind cladding, which can be anything from stone to glass to metal; in other cases, such as timber-frame or brick buildings, the structure and the cladding are the same. In both, the fabric of the building is exposed to the elements and 'ages' as a result. Buildings, specifically domestic ones, are often intended to remain in place for 50 years at least, and therefore the choice of materials used on the outside is particularly important. Old buildings may be perceived as more valuable because they have stood the test of time and have attained character through the weathering process. This applies to everything from the humble beach hut with its flaking paint to the stone edifices of nineteenth-century architecture that form much of the streetscapes of European towns and cities. This perception may be accompanied by the suspicion that modern materials are either cheap and throw-away or monumental and austere.

Thus, the choice of materials is important not just at a functional level but also at an emotional one; the combination of different materials can add a richness of associations. For example, there is a current trend for cladding houses in timber, even in the most urban locations, suggesting a softer and more natural environment. Indeed the way these surfaces weather is an important consideration, reflecting the passage of time as traces and marks are deposited and imprinted on to the timber. The

Top left The Susuki House appears to be propped up on the street side by a forked column and to be perching on a wedge on the other. The graphic nature of the façade lends the house a particularly cute character.
Centre left Only a few pieces of loose furniture inhabit the main living space; spare chairs are hung on the wall to keep them out of the way. *Below left* The inside of the concrete box reveals a further container that holds the bedroom, which is lit from a series of ribbon windows.
Opposite above In the Ta House by Kei' Ichie Irie, the materiality of the panelled exterior wall is emphasized by the tree that has been left in place beside it.
Opposite below Behind the screen wall large glass windows and light wood flooring create an airy, linear living space.

choice of materials is also important when considering sustainability issues, an increasingly critical factor for many architects and clients today.

Baggy House sits in a stunning location at Baggy Point, North Devon, England. Designed by the London office of Hudson Featherstone Architects, it is an expressively rendered collection of forms connected by a central chimney feature. The house owes something to the traditions of twentieth-century architects Charles Rennie Mackintosh and Charles Voysey, but closer inspection reveals a more hybrid approach to materials and details. To one side, overlooking the sea, there is an open glazed corner which is protected by an overhanging copper roof. As the salty air oxidizes the copper it turns green and its colour and surface texture will continue to change over time.

Transparency The materiality of Katsuyasu Kishigami's Imazato House in Kagawa Prefecture, Japan, is sublime in its simplicity. This diagrammatic box is clad in galvanized steel on two sides and translucent polycarbonate on the other two. At

night the effect is that of a lantern, the whole building acting as a beacon on the street, the material appearing almost to dissolve into the dark; by day it appears far more solid and dumb. While the use of this cladding system was dictated by cost – it is most often found in agricultural buildings – the result is suprisingly elegant.

Glass is used extensively in house construction to create a sense of space and light, although it is in fact very heavy. While one might like to consider using huge plate-glass sheets, the size of one sheet of glass has limitations, often dictated by the transportation options to the site. In many modern homes it is not just the amount of glass that creates a sense of space, but how the light itself is moderated and brought inside. A north-facing rooflight will illuminate a room evenly while an east-facing window might capture the morning sun directly.

The perception of lightness is not simply achieved through maximum glazing but by carefully engineering out heavy structural elements, which often means using steel framing to carry the weight. Chunky window frames, such as the unfortunate

UPVC variety, lead to an overall sense of heaviness, especially when compared to the slimline elegance of a Georgian glazing bar. There is a catch, however: as legislation changes, encouraging new buildings to be made with greater thermal capacity, it is not always possible to use the amount of glass that might be desired. Double-glazing can be the answer, though even this allows some heat to escape. As more attention is paid to environmental issues, architecture will necessarily have to change and new building materials and technologies will shape the homes of the future.

Aesthetics and style

In his book *Towards a New Architecture* (1923), Le Corbusier wrote, 'Architecture has nothing to do with the various styles. The styles of Louis XIV or Gothic are to architecture what a feather is on a woman's hat; it is sometimes pretty, though not always, and never anything more…' His own view was that the 'spirit of the age' was more than simply a style, it was a cast of mind. This sentiment was a reaction to the lingering influence of late nineteenth-century style

and its excesses of decoration which persisted over much of post-war Europe – a modern way of life was yet to be expressed within people's homes.

The history of architecture may be seen as the triumph of one aesthetic or preference over another; in the nineteenth century it was the battle between Classical and Gothic architecture. This is illustrated in the proposed designs for the new Houses of Parliament in London which were drawn up in both styles, though the basic structure was exactly the same. The façades in one were clad in columns in the Classical style while the other featured Gothic stone tracery. In the end, after much heated debate, the Gothic style, as proposed by AWN Pugin, won the vote as it was considered to be the more democratic of the two, in tune with the pious religious principles of the day. Today there is perhaps similar confusion over which way to turn but there does not appear to be an easy answer to the question 'What next?' When we can choose from the pick'n'mix of historical styles to conjure up any age we like, that we should aspire to live in a totally modern world remains a minority choice.

Above At night, the gently glowing façades of the Imazato House by Katsuyasu Kishigami create a compelling ambience around it. Opposite Beneath the verdigrised copper roof of Hudson Featherstone Architects' Baggy House, the glazed walls of the south and west elevations can be dropped into the ground to open up the interior to the sea air.

Old or new? The option before us now appears to be a simplistic one between old and new. Situations where contrasting architectures should not be juxtaposed are few and far between: the argument is no longer about which style is more worthy or true, but rather one of taste. While on the surface this liberalization of possibility seems a good thing, it does not give any guide as to what may be more appropriate or better in the long run. Hence we live in a world where it seems safer to build in a manner that has already proved successful than to be experimental. The majority of people seem to feel more connected, literally 'at home', in environments that look old and traditional and exude a sense of timelessness.

In 1933 the English poet and architectural critic John Betjeman wrote a book entitled *Ghastly Good Taste*, which is subtitled *A Depressing Story of the Rise and Fall of English Architecture*. Here he expressed his horror at the speed of change in the modern world and the architecture that stemmed from it. Betjeman too seemed to find a source of conflict in his admiration for old, historic buildings and his attempts at coming to terms with the new architecture. His book comes with a delightful pull-out drawing demonstrating changing styles and expressions, ending in the present day with lumpen buildings and chaotic street scenes.

In the twenty-first century we seem to have accepted notions of contradiction, of new buildings sitting next to old, in our cities but not necessarily in our homes and their environs. Whole towns and villages have been built as studies in their local vernacular architecture, perhaps in an attempt to defy this ever-changing 'civilization'.

One of the best-known examples of traditionalist architecture in England is at Poundbury on the outskirts of Dorchester. Designed by urban architect Leon Krier and begun in 1993, the project is famously endorsed by the Prince of Wales and has a number of highly vocal and evangelistic residents. The scheme is intended to represent the epitome of traditional English life and each house has been designed slightly differently to create the impression that the streetscape has evolved over time. While on the surface Poundbury looks like a quaint rural village, it is in fact a peculiar mix of wilful aesthetics and social interfaces: you cannot, for instance, choose what colour to paint your front door. Cars are kept out of some streets and garages are grouped together in buildings that look like converted barns. One of the buildings that looks like a large home is, in fact, divided up into flats, thereby mimicking the trend for the (often poor) conversion of old buildings – a gesture that can only be interpreted as perverse.

Taste versus fashion The conundrum between what is considered architectural and what is homely could, today, be defined as a taste issue. The modern homes that we see in the media are tantalizing and seductive but, when it comes down to it, the choice between clean lines and rustic textures is too extreme: most people want both. This lack of whole-hearted enthusiasm for the modern may, in part, have to do with the continuing perception that 'modern style' is too minimal and uncomfortable. It is fortunate, therefore, that there are more choices to be made. Another factor could be a certain elitist architectural conspiracy which dictates that good taste is defined by a number of key components and materials. These include large expanses of glass, grey metalwork, white render and timber cladding on the outsides of buildings; while within, the accepted style is for oak flooring, white-painted walls, stainless-steel door handles and recessed downlights. These combined elements could be described as 'architectural style', something that has come to be seen as a kind of a cliché. In many ways this is no different from the Modernists, not least because they too did not recognize that they had invented a style – the last thing they intended to do. That said, there are enough designers who are not afraid of colonizing their buildings with furniture and clutter and who have a strong sense of what it means to construct a home.

Architecture and design have always adapted over the course of time, changes that are well documented in the plethora of books on the subject. In the past few decades the rate of change has been ever increasing. Intellectuals have indulged in naming the various movements, or styles, from Post-Modernism to Deconstruction, from Modern Vernacular to Hi-tech. The value of this pigeon-holing is debateable, and has narrowed the gap between building and fashion. The media taste-machine generates new genres and imagery every season, bamboozling the culturally aware public with choices. A well-known colour-prediction magazine chooses a palette of colours it thinks will be fashionable 18 months in advance and it is no surprise to find that its forecasts are usually realized: manufacturers are eager to get designs off the

Another famous example of a new/old town is Celebration in Miami, Florida, United States, which was set up by the Disney Corporation. The town appears quaint and historic but it is all completely new. There are resonances of *The Truman Show*, the 1998 film that features a character born into a soap-opera who does not know that he is living in a synthetic fantasy world where his every movement is being filmed and relayed to the public. The price of living in Celebration is that you must be vetted beforehand, and that the home you choose to live in has been built from a pattern book. Among many architects and designers there is a feeling that this way of life allows little chance for self-expression and that communities manufactured in this way cannot ultimately be self-sustaining.

Above left This tasteful kitchen/living space is the epitome of late twentieth-century style: a timber floor, white walls and a classic Modernist chair peeping from behind the door. *Below left* In another interior the same modern palette has been used but the design incorporates interesting dynamic forms: the staircase has been wrapped in timber, creating a fashionable 'intervention'. *Opposite* This development in Graham Square, Glasgow, by McKeown Alexander graphically illustrates the conflict between old and new architecture. The historic façade has been kept in place and appears to be propped up by the new housing behind it – a gesture that is perhaps a little mannered.

drawing board and on to the factory floor in time
for the new season. The same is not quite true of
architecture, partly because the timescale for
building is much longer, though buildings and
interiors serve as backdrops for fashion-industry
advertising. The building is a product that can be
bought and styled just like anything else.

In the course of the 1990s one group of artists
and architects in London known as FAT – Fashion,
Architecture and Taste – developed their own
commentary, merging stylistic observations with a
wry sense of irony. A house in East London recently
completed by Sean Griffiths is a collage of styles:
New England clapboard meets urban warehouse.
This approach is highly individual and playful, paying
no attention to perceived notions of good taste and
accepted rhetoric. The only problem with this highly
individual approach is that it requires a setting to
react against. In other words, it stands out from the
drab brick council blocks and light-industrial
buildings in the neighbourhood. It is therefore a very
particular model for developing ideas about new
housing which relies on creating an individual
expression in a sea of sameness. Yet this idea of

collaging elements seems to be an essential part of
the culture we now live in and there is no doubt
that we can 'read' the façade of the house, thus
triggering a whole set of associations and memories,
which adds to the richness of the built environment.

Judgement day Understanding the difference
between architecture and building is critical to the
decisions that inform the design of houses and
housing. Clearly both activities involve building, so
the answer must lie in how the results are evaluated
and cherished. Firstly the way in which houses are
built is supremely important – will they last, are they
adaptable, do they inspire the occupier? Secondly
one has to look at the broader cultural aspects of
society and see if the design is looking forward, from
the ways in which people are living their lives now
to how they might live them in the future. Thirdly,
the design should reflect the local conditions such
as the weather, the streetscape and the wider
context. We remain fascinated by what we cannot
have, and if we have the confidence to be more
daring there is the reward of surprise, originality
and delight that pioneering offers.

3. The Changing Face of the City

The Changing Face of the City
Familiarity and Difference

Urban fabric

When looking at new homes in the city, whether in the centre or within the suburbs, it is often difficult to understand the circumstances that led to their construction. The concept of the masterplan seems grandiose and dated, though in many ways it has simply been replaced by the term development. Most major cities already have an infrastructure that has grown up as they have expanded. Therefore it is only when a building becomes redundant or damaged that it is possible to replace it. In most inner cities there are few empty plots on which to build as small, uninhabited sites are cherished as parks and public spaces – you

have only to think of Manhattan's 'pocket parks'. Even on the outskirts of the city where there appears to be available space, there are restrictions that prevent the eating-up of countryside and development zones have to be negotiated. Yet with expanding populations and the requirement for new homes, more radical propositions are being considered.

Suburbia A loaded term that often carries pejorative connotations, 'suburbia' conjures up swathes of low-density housing that all looks the same, with little sense of place. Of course this is a generalization; there are incredibly sought-after

suburban neighbourhoods where every house has an individual 'signature'. Yet the very word 'sub-urban' implies that it is beyond the city, but does not quite count as the countryside.

Suburbs are a relatively new phenomenon, springing up after the Industrial Revolution as a response to housing shortages in the big cities. Land outside city boundaries was developed to create new housing, fulfilling the widespread desire among the middle classes to escape from the dirty, over-crowded streets of the inner cities. A great deal of importance was placed on the 'greenness' of these new locations and they were promoted as being good places to bring up families. The development of transport infrastructure in the nineteenth century meant that these out-of-town areas could be easily accessed and so was born a new model of inhabitation which is now recognized globally.

What differentiates suburbia from either a city, town or its rural counterpart is that it has been built from scratch, often around a transport interchange.

The golden age of suburbia in Europe was perhaps the inter-war years, when development took place at an extraordinary rate. Streets of semi-detached houses were built, with front gardens and rows of trees. They had a scale that could be mistaken as 'villagey', yet it might be miles to the nearest shop or pub, because these homes were not in the heart of a village or town; they were on the edge of a city. Today there is a tendency for services such as shops, restaurants and entertainment to be situated at out-of-town shopping centres or malls which can only be accessed by car.

The unchanged formula If suburbia is so big, why is it the setting for so few adventurous, experimental or modern homes? Planner Paul Barker believes that suburbs give the majority of people the kinds of homes they want and as such are despised by architects. This perhaps touches on the core of the problem: very little suburban housing is designed by architects, but instead is initiated by

Above The potential to subvert the monotony of suburbia is illustrated by this radical French project by Lacoste-Stevenson. Timber-frame houses are clad in waterproof membranes and PVC sheeting which is printed with brightly coloured designs. It is a stylistic, almost fashion-orientated approach that challenges the everday streetscape.

developers who prefer not to take risks in terms of style and design – the caricature of neat, identical houses, well-tended front gardens and family cars in driveways still holds true. There is little scope for radical new buildings because the chance of an individual finding a small plot of land in an area of permitted development is very slim, unless a plot is created in the boundary between two other homes or an old building is replaced by a new one. Even adding an extension to an existing suburban house may require planning permission. It could be argued that this is one of the reasons why suburbia just seems to get older and often more decrepit, as it does not yet have to regenerate itself. As houses reach the end of their natural lives – of, say, 100 to 150 years – this will all have to change. Tastes move on and if a house is sturdy it can accept modifications to bring it into line with new lifestyles and preferences.

Many houses we choose to think of as typically suburban have already been modified to some extent; the heating system will have been upgraded, a new kitchen fitted, another bathroom squeezed in, new decor applied. In larger houses the attic may have been converted into another room or the garage made into a playroom. Some owners may even have approached an architect to create additional space by building an extension. Today there are some notable exceptions to the suburban rule that show we no longer share the requirements of an older generation brought up in cellular rooms that established the boundaries of cooking, eating, living and sleeping. There are many excellent examples of extensions and conversions resulting in much more contemporary living arrangements and spaces. But the results are only partially new. The challenge is to create a new model for suburban living that is associated with a modern way of life.

New homes in old settings The contrast between the existing urban fabric and the new is always striking in suburbia, precisely because so much of it looks the same. The traditional Victorian street in London has been the scene of recent changes, an example of which is the new home known as 1A, designed by Mike Tonkin. Having spent much of his working life in Hong Kong, his

interest in different forms of domestic inhabitation displays an Eastern sensibility. Much of the thinking in this house reflects the brief of the clients, a creative couple who both wanted individual studios and who were open to the idea that new kinds of spaces would encourage an alternative way of living.

The long thin plot can be seen as a container for a series of inhabited objects which are laid out along the edges of the site. The elevation on to the street is an opaque, double-height glass façade, rendered white on both sides. The double-height volume on the street side contains living space below and bedrooms above. The internal layout has a void at its centre, unlike a typical house which sits as an object surrounded by garden. This courtyard is filled with an open reflecting pool, along one side of which is a string of enfilade rooms including a small studio, the toilets and a dining niche. At the far end another glazed studio room completes the cloister.

The whole building has been planned on a modular grid and fabricated mainly from timber; throughout, the lightness of the construction is celebrated and individual elements appear to float. The use of water as a reference to nature is more meditative and tranquil than a pastoral idyll. Views across the water allow elusive glimpses into rooms which are denied in traditional houses that have closed doors. The haunting quality of this beautiful bespoke home is reinforced by the fact that it is so different from its neighbours in almost every way, even though functionally it is the same – just a place to live and work.

Another white box is the Drop House designed by Anthony Hudson which is situated in an altogether more leafy suburb of London in Hertfordshire. Visually it could not be more different from its red-brick, pitched-roofed neighbour. Here the house is understood as a white sculptural object which appears literally to have been dropped into place. It is a collision of English Modernism and fashionable American East Coast Brutalism. 'Drop' also refers to an egg-like object that is visible from the street at first-floor level through an opening in the wall; it contains a playful bathroom at the upper level and a utility room lower down. The use of this organic, three-dimensional form within the ordered geometry of the house creates a series of surprising leftover spaces which are inhabited in a variety of ways. The guest rooms are on the lower-ground floor which opens up on to a garden, while the main living area is a double-height space connected to the kitchen, a study and a specialist audio-visual room.

While there is no sense of the house being ordinary, it still maintains the functionality of a typical suburban family home. The living and sleeping quarters are separated and the setting allows easy access to the open garden space as well as to smaller raised terraces and balconies, which trap the sun but are not overlooked by the next-door houses. The final twist is that the house has been designed to recycle every last drop of water and so fulfils all the interpretations of its cartoon-like name.

A more hybrid approach to the question of its suburban context is found in a newly constructed

Above The Drop House by Anthony Hudson breaks the mould of historicist suburban models by celebrating its own autonomy. The white box contains an egg-shaped object which appears to float above the walls.

Opposite above The tranquillity of the internal courtyard of Mike Tonkin's House 1A is amplified by the still reflecting pool.

Opposite below From outside, House 1A reads as a pared-down cubic volume set back from the street. In front there is an elegant canopy protecting the entrance way. The white painted finish of this house and its neighbour is a unifying factor.

house in Berlin by Peter Herrle. Opposite sits a polite rendered building with red clay roof tiles and modern windows framed by slatted shutters – it is perhaps only the scale of development that is shared by the two houses. The new building sits among tall, spindly trees. From a distance the form of the house could be mistaken for something more traditional; it is clad in timber and has a pitched roof, giving it a shed-like quality. On closer inspection, however, the cladding is seen to have sophisticated horizontal detailing and the plan of the building is more unusual than first imagined.

The layout is divided in two by the staircase that connects the ground and first floors. The pitched roof element contains living accommodation while the smaller slice on the other side of the stair contains the services, including bathrooms, closet space and kitchen. This zone is expressed as a concrete box on the outside. The horizontal larch cladding of the barn structure becomes an infill panel on the short elevation of the service wing. Windows have shutters that are top-hung so that they form a sun shade when open and disappear completely when closed. The slot connecting the two built elements is glazed over. There is a little self-contained apartment on the ground floor accessed from the back.

Within, the palette of timber and concrete continues and the staircase has a wonderful sense of being both inside and outside, as it is clad in timber on one side and concrete on the other, with cantilevered concrete treads. There is no question that this is a very clever little building, playing a handful of architectural cards. As a home it appears functional yet elegant.

In the city of Utrecht in The Netherlands, maverick architects MVRDV have built the Double House on a patch of land surrounded by period housing that overlooks a nineteenth-century park. The house has been imagined as a box and is inhabited by two families. The way the box has been carved up is reflected on the façade by a collaged series of transparent openings, windows and voids. From the street you can literally read the houses and understand what is going on behind each window. The division between the two is not simply

a vertical wall as in a standard semi-detached house; rather it is a three-dimensional plane reflecting a more complex inter-relationship between the families. The architects describe the house as an intellectually ambitious project which, for them, graphically illustrates the negotiated and uncertain boundaries that exist between one neighbour and another. Their approach could be seen as being too public and too experimental, yet the result is a striking, animated composition that actually looks like a fun place to be.

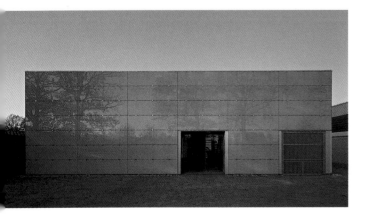

In the nearby city of Almelo, the opposite tactic was taken by architect Dirk Jan Postel. His minimal house presents a screen wall to the street. It is punctured by two identical openings, one for the front door and the other for a garage. The exterior is made from large sheets of fritted glass which have been sandblasted with a pattern. These are clipped on to a timber frame that is not visible from the outside. The opaque glass façade encloses three sides of the building; the fourth, south-facing façade is clad in cedar and glazed with clear glass. There is also a minimalist sunroom at the back of the house in the

Opposite **This house by Peter Herrle separates the programme of accommodation into living spaces and service spaces, creating a graphic architectural statement.** *Above* **The Double House by MVRDV, shown here just before completion, is a volumetric jigsaw puzzle that plays games of transparency, structural gymnastics and composition.** *Left* **The use of timber on the rear façade of Dirk Jan Postel's minimalist house softens its austerity.** *Below left* **The front façade reflects its surroundings, looking more like a billboard than a home.**

form of a glazed box. Inside, a logical series of divisions creates an open-plan living space on the ground floor and four cellular rooms upstairs; the master bedroom opens on to the conservatory roof. Overall the house has a chilling effect. It is clinical, neat and clever and the inhabitant would have to be someone who was happy to live a clutter-free life.

On the other side of the world in Sydney, there are a surprisingly large number of Victorian suburban houses, built by the incumbent expatriates. They display the familiar trademarks of nineteenth-century domestic architecture: pitched roofs, porches over the front doors, painted timber bargeboarding. Within these historic suburban neighbourhoods there are gaps that provide ideal opportunities for constructing new types of housing. In the district of Redfern, architects Engelen Moore have built a house between two others which has been conceived as a homage to minimalist living. The scale of the street is maintained, though the language of the house owes much to the Modernist tradition of the white box, and from the outside one might mistakenly think that it is an industrial shed nestling amongst the traditional brick buildings. Inside there are 6m (20ft) high ceilings which give an inspiring sense of scale and space. The end elevation is an impressive glass wall which actually folds away so that in the summer the space is completely open to the elements. The concrete floor, which has underfloor heating for winter, continues outside and folds down into an elegant lap pool. The bedroom is housed on a mezzanine that overlooks the main space, enhancing the open-plan experience.

The driving force behind this idealistic project was the budget – it had to be as cheap as possible. This was achieved by using steel portal frames infilled with concrete block to create an unadorned, functional enclosure that is extremely flexible. The building, in effect, is a shell that can be fitted out in whatever style the owner chooses. The result must surely be a highly convincing example of how to create maximum space with minimum money. The house remains curiously iconic, partly because it is so photogenic – it is always summer here, with sunlight reflecting off the surface of the pool.

City limits It has recently been argued that there is a new kind of suburbia that seeks to define the 'edge of a city'. The middle-aged spread that happens to cities is the result of cheaper land prices outside city centres, the proximity of transport interchanges or lack of urban regeneration initiatives. The result is density without intensity. Logic suggests that there must be a line where a city ends, yet in reality it remains elusive. Is it where the last building stands, or where you can no longer hear the traffic or see the buildings? Current urban planning seems to be in favour of preventing expansion and reclaiming these edges as part of the city proper rather than a fade-out zone. In his book, *Edge of a City* (1991), architect Steven Holl describes the horizon as a recurring theme in his own work. He seeks to contain the sprawl that occurs on the perimeter of cities and to create spaces rather than a series of objects. Though many of his projects remain conceptual or unrealized, such as his 'Spatial Retaining Bars' for Phoenix Arizona and his masterplan for the Porta Vittoria in Milan, he has initiated debates about the phenomenon of urban sprawl, a problem which had been ignored for too long. Suburbia is being rethought as a place for new development and growth, not only in terms of building but also politics, economics and sustainability.

New cities In some parts of the world there are whole cities that are essentially suburban, with no critical mass at their centres, based around the motor car as the primary means of transport. This kind of development largely grew up in the post-war period in areas where land values were cheap. The desire to own an individual house and garden, as opposed to an apartment or condominium, led to widespread, low-rise growth. However this model of urban planning is now seen as less sustainable as petrol prices rise and the ecological effects of CO_2 emission are felt. In the city of Los Angeles streets of low-rise housing fold over the gently rolling foothills around Hollywood and beyond, all connected by ribbons of tarmac. Cheap lots meant that people could afford to build in a style that suited them and here the legacy of contemporary architecture is

Right This monolithic block by Wendell Burnett Architects balances above a boundary wall overlooking the city of Los Angeles in the United States. By night the large framed balcony looks like a vast television screen projecting the domestic drama of the home out to the city.

seen on every street corner. Today there are some fine examples of experimental new homes.

In his Canyon Residence, set into the hillside overlooking Los Angeles, architect Steven Ehrlich has created a luxurious sculptural home. The concept for the building is based on a series of vertical stuccoed retaining walls which hold fireplaces, services and stairs. These are connected by a series of horizontal rafts that make up the floors and ceilings; where they project on to the outside as canopies, they are clad in copper. The building is carefully sited between a number of existing trees which lends a sense of permanence and belonging. A number of terraces form outside rooms, negotiating the boundary between inside and out. It owes much in its appearance to the massing of Frank Lloyd Wright's homes and to the legacy of a more brutal Modernism. As the house gently steps down the site the flow of space is manipulated, from the 6m (20ft) high living space down to the much lower bedrooms. From the back the house looks isolated, but from the road one is

aware of many other houses, similarly set into the undergrowth, enjoying this urban/rural location. The owner of the house wishes to remain anonymous and this is perhaps reflected in the front entrance, which is a closed, formal composition giving away little of the grand spaces within.

In Japan new cities have also developed as a series of low-rise suburban neighbourhoods; again, with a curiously homogeneous feeling, although the style of individual buildings can vary enormously. This development is largely due to two factors; firstly, the lack of easily developed land — much of Japan is mountainous, so development is concentrated on the lower coastal areas; and secondly, the threat of earthquakes, which has led to legislation restricting building heights and forms of construction. It is usual to find that houses do not touch one another in case one should collapse and damage its neighbour.

In one such neighbourhood in Nagoya, architects Takeyama and Amorphe recently completed a house for a single person. The site is a strip between

various other houses that appear bland and unremarkable, taking the standard form of grey-tiled pitched roofs and beige rendered façades. The new house makes a statement by not conforming either to the local context or to any traditional forms of Japanese construction, proposing a completely different aesthetic. A square concrete tower anchors the corner of the site and is connected to the double-height, metal-clad body of the house which is a long gallery space. The tower contains a Tatami room in the basement – a traditional layout of woven mats that can be used as a prayer room or for tea ceremonies – two bathrooms on the next two floors and a terrace on the roof. The main living accommodation is found in the curious folded geometry of the 'barn'. The two are linked by a glazed balcony element, allowing a connection between the bedroom and bathroom. The end elevation is clad in the same oxidized red steel that also frames the front door. Above, and to one side, a simple square window is the only clue to the domesticity behind. A small reflecting pool sits in the hard-landscaped area next to the timber dividing wall and a cluster of mature bamboo shoots. Within, the space is finished in a palette of hard materials: concrete and terracotta on the floor, white-painted walls and a steel-and-glass stair and mezzanine.

The overall impact is powerful mainly because the building does not look like a traditional house and therefore challenges the status of others around it. The language of the building is also modern and minimal; there are windows and doors, but they are more industrial than domestic in feel, and the main space has more in common with a contemporary art gallery than a living room. Yet as an experiment that seeks to define a new kind of home for the single individual it is remarkably bold, suggesting to its neighbours that not all houses have to look the same.

In the thick of it The redevelopment of inner cities relies on complex, shifting patterns of inhabitation and changes of use. Areas that were once designated as light-industrial zones, such as the meatpacking district in New York or the warehouse area of Shoreditch in East London have found themselves at the epicentre of 'cool' urban regeneration. As manufacturing moves out of central locations to more accessible modern sites, buildings become vacant and low rents attract bohemian groups who are eager to live centrally and do not mind living in such run-down environments. These neighbourhoods become slowly gentrified to the point at which the original inhabitants can no longer afford the rents and more wealthy types move in. This colonization is not a new phenomenon, but it demonstrates that regeneration is not something that can be foreseen or designed – it can just happen. Both of the above examples have been rebranded as 'lifestyle' locations made attractive by the proliferation of bars, restaurants and housing. Once the area appears able to sustain its value, the developers move in and begin to knock down buildings and construct new complexes – often residential – to maximize their returns. It is within this context that we look at those who do not necessarily wish to be part of a new trend or initiative, and who are willing to stick their necks out to find a slice of land they can call their own.

Above Designed for a single person, this highly wrought Japanese house by Takeyama and Amorphe demonstrates that spatial and programmatic complexity can be squeezed on to a small site. *Opposite* At night the transparent façade of the Small House by Kazuyo Sejima reveals the living arrangements of those inside should they so choose. The central staircase, which is also a structural device, climbs up the centre of the building.

Tall and skinny Often the only sites left on which to build an individual dwelling in a city are those forgotten slots that were once garages or parking spaces. Traditionally these pieces of land have not been seen as valuable, but as house prices increase and other options narrow, the idea of developing small houses to fit them becomes more attractive. This is especially true in Tokyo where housing in city centres is at a premium. Here the last ten years have seen much development in the housing market and, as engineering becomes more sophisticated, high-rise, earthquake-proof towers provide new alternatives. But not everyone wants to live in a tower block.

The aptly named Small House (see p.75), designed by architect Kazuyo Sejima, occupies a 36 sq m (388 sq ft) footprint in downtown Tokyo. It is reached via a cul-de-sac in the heart of a fashionable commercial area. The four-storey building is an unusual faceted form, with every floor a slightly different shape. In part this is a simple reflection of the calculations used to create the maximum permissible envelope. The exterior is clad in standing-seam galvanized steel and glass. Inside, a spiral stair provides the vertical circulation and the functional elements lie around the edges. The ground floor is the main family room, with a half-basement below containing a bedroom and toilet; the second floor contains the kitchen and dining room with a 3.5m (11½ft) high ceiling; and the top floor houses a Japanese-style soaking tub and opens on to a roof terrace that commands great views over the city. Designed for a small family, the bedroom is at present used by all, though it is imagined that in time the daughter will use the family room as a bedroom. At night the whole house is illuminated from within and appears completely transparent from the most private aspect, though still opaque from the front.

As a structure, the house has been highly innovative. The main staircase acts as a supporting column which is braced in a way to withstand quake tremors along with the four poured-concrete floor slabs. The cranky form of the building perhaps suggests that it may already have been subject to a quake and been deformed as a result. Sejima feels that the expression she has devised is an example of

Left A slot house by Joe Hagan in London's Golden Lane is a clear example of how a sliver of land can be built on and extruded upwards to create a mini seven-storey tower. The street façade is a simple steel frame infilled with glass panels; as it returns, however, the wall is clad in rustic timber planks.

Opposite left Another slot house in Japan by Architecture Produce Association makes its mark on the streetscape by giving nothing away. A winding staircase disappears into a void behind a double-height white screen, above which are etched-glass windows.

Opposite centre The private interior is a light and airy living space on several levels.

form following function, albeit a very personal and wilful interpretation. It could be said that the benefit of building in Tokyo is that, despite the constriction of space, there is no aesthetic style police, so even a small home has the freedom to be individual. What it lacks in space it gains in character.

A similarly constricted site, a small yard on to a main road, was used to build a tall house on Golden Lane in East London. Originally architect Joe Hagan intended to build the house for himself, but later decided to sell the site on with planning permission. It was bought by a client who retained Hagan's main ideas but decided to introduce an elevator into the seven-storey building despite the small floor area. The main façade has floor-to-ceiling glazing set out

in regular bays, emphasizing the restrictions of the plot. As the building rises out of the site, the longer, side elevation is seen to be clad in rough-sawn timber, stained dark brown, culminating in a roof terrace. The effect of this façade is challenging, offering a rustic sensibility to a street where large billboards occupy much of the neighbouring main road. Next to the front door a galvanized zinc trough is filled with bamboo that rustles in the breeze, casting shadows on to the etched glass window. The spaces within are handled with a Zen-like simplicity. White walls and timber floors connect the vertically stacked spaces, and light from the large windows helps the spaces appear airy and generous. The project creates a housing opportunity from a

towards the top of the house. The base is dark, almost black, with a carved timber front door inset to one side. Like all infill sites there is only one public elevation and in this case it is iconic.

The plan of the interior is also surprising. The body of the house is a rectangle with the two flanks taking up the squinched geometry of the site, to create a trianglar space. A steel stair enclosed in glass threads its way up the building, giving on to rooms sited at half-landings up to the fourth floor. This cross-section creates a dynamic interaction between the internal spaces, suggesting that their function and inhabitation overlap. The stair also acts as a lightwell connecting all the rooms vertically, unlike the traditional model of a townhouse in which the stair is isolated. Light from the long windows casts an ever-changing pattern on to the neutral walls, emphasizing the abstract nature of the interior. Despite the limitations of the site, this house offers an entirely different way of life from its neighbours.

Compare this to a similar strategy employed by architects Herzog and de Meuron on a larger scale in their apartment building in Basle, Switzerland. The site was 23m (73ft) in length but only 6.3m (20½) wide. In order to create a plan for each apartment that brought in natural light, an eccentric courtyard was created towards the back of the site. The most striking aspect of this building is its uncompromisingly graphic façade. There are six storeys of floor-to-ceiling glass, divided up regularly, each with a veil of cast-iron shutters to cut itself off from the street. The metal grilles are made up of wavy bars, allowing light into the interior, filtering it as though through a curtain. By day, when all the shutters are closed, the building appears fortress-like; but by night, and when the shutters are open, it has a magical presence.

The ground floor of the building leads through to the entrance of the small Swiss Fire Fighting Museum, with an elevator connecting all the floors.

Left Inside Architecture Studio's Parisian house, light filters through the windows of the façade and is projected on to surfaces deep inside the home, creating an ever-changing cinematic experience. Opposite Two floor-to-ceiling glass panels form the main façade of this house on Club Row in London. The balcony on the roof of the first floor acts as an outside room, making the most of the limited space available.

space that was no bigger than a suburban garage and serves as a model of how extruded buildings can make excellent living spaces. In addition, this densification contributes to the life of the city, recycling pockets of leftover space.

The main design challenge faced when building a tall house is the circulation. The staircase in so many houses plays a purely functional role, whereas in a 'slot house' it must often perform a number of tasks: it must give structural stability and provide a place for storage, but also be transparent in order to minimize its impact as an object. A recent house in Paris by Architecture Studio (see p. 77), set within the fabric of rue Robert Blanche, demonstrates a highly versatile staircase arrangement. Externally, the house is immediately striking as the façade angles back, held within two white, curved 'bookends'. This single gesture sets it apart from its traditional white-stuccoed neighbours. The façade is clad in dark tropical timber with a hierarchy of horizontally slotted windows, whose syncopation changes

The actual apartments are L-shaped at the back, with a linear kitchen located in the smaller return of the 'L' overlooking the courtyard and trees beyond. The rear aspect is south-facing and fully glazed, so external timber blinds can be lowered to gain privacy and shade. The interiors are fitted out simply with timber-strip floors and white walls. The building is topped by a polite, set-back penthouse. Overall the project demonstrates the ingenuity of a well-considered plan; the architects have taken delight in considering a seemingly simple, flat façade and turning it into a building with a character that is felt from within as well as outside.

On a more modest scale, a house on Club Row in East London, designed by architect partners Howard Carter and Sarah Cheeseman of Thinking Space as a home for themselves, represents a canny intervention in the city. The site had been empty for 50 years, seemingly too small to be developed. The complexity of site conditions and next-door buildings led to the creation of one large space, 8m (26ft) tall, with galleries around it. A new basement, lit from above, was built to provide additional accommodation, while the flat roof contains a terrace and a glazed light to the void below. From the outside the building looks odd, sitting next to a robust redbrick warehouse with its original terracotta detailing. The house is made of sandy coloured brick and glass, the full-height metal windows are dark grey, and the glazed balcony edge to the roof is taller than usually found, suggesting an outdoor room on the top of the house. The space within is a three-dimensional jigsaw in blond timber and white-painted walls. The bedroom is part open-plan with a bathroom created from awkward spaces at the back. The project is recognizably 'house-like' and manages to suggest that the inhabited area is bigger than the confines of the site would suggest.

Nearby, off a busy arterial road, there is another house built by an architect for his family. William Russell's building is an extremely robust vision of concrete, steel and glass — materials that reflect the gritty urban nature of the neighbourhood. Nevertheless the sculptural manipulation of the corner site has led to the creation of a fascinating

cubic object, completely different from its Victorian
brick neighbours. A combination of full-height, clear
and etched double-glazed units and zinc cladding
leaves few clues as to the use of the building; only
the odd glimpse afforded by the slot window into
the bedrooms gives the home away. Unlike the
house at Club Row the interior has been left in a
basic, unfinished state. Raw concrete stairs and
floors lend a mean 'gallery installation' feeling to the
space, which is partly a reflection of the low budget
yet is also part of the work in progress that such a
project represents. Over time new elements and
finishes can be introduced into the interior, surfaces
can be reclad – it is all part of the experiment.

Perched on top Another tactic for finding
more inhabitable space is to build on top of
something that is already there. This may involve the
conversion of an attic or loft, or grafting on a new
structure entirely. This kind of architecture is often
referred to as parasitic, as it literally feeds off the
existing body of the building, utilizing its structure
and tapping into its network of pipes and wires. An
inventive example of this approach has been
constructed on the roof of a former laundry right in
the centre of Vienna in Austria. Designed by Gregor
Eichinger of EOK architects, the tiny space is
flooded with light and is remarkably tightly planned
within a 35 sq m (376 $^1\!/_2$ sq ft) floorplate. The design
ensures that elements are multifunctional, increasing
their efficiency to free up space for living in. The
island kitchen is a low, angled element behind which
is a shower and a folding stainless steel door hiding
the toilet. The wet area for bathing is demarcated by
a blue mosaic floor, with the plumbing integrated
into a metal column. As an optimistic but poetic act
a skylight has been situated above the shower and
can be opened to allow in the natural elements. The
bedroom is a separate room on the other side of
the chimney breast wall of the main building below.
A large, heavy, bi-folding window can be operated
electronically to open the main room up and, in true
James Bond style, another button moves the lower
pane of glass forwards to become the balcony edge.
This fascination with technology transforms the tiny
flat into a box of tricks, which can only be operated

by those in the know. There are three very different types of window, lead detailing on the roof and a series of access decks, steps and railings at the very top. This combination of old and new is a collage of architectural elements and forms that hints at the sophisticated world inside. Outside, the building is invisible from the street and can only be seen at rooftop level from neighbouring windows. The result is more a conglomeration of elements than a slick, designed object. It takes on the language of objects added to the roofs.

A much more purist solution was deployed by minimalist architect Mark Guard when he created a rooftop apartment in Paris. The original site was a 32 sq m (344 sq ft) construction on top of an eight-storey, 1930s department store in the centre of the city. Outside, a terrace was constructed in front of a new folding glass wall, which is partly protected by a canopy. Inside, three free-standing boxes house

functional elements such as the washing machine, wardrobes and the television. The bedroom area can be closed up if necessary and there is a sofa bed for visitors. The door to the bathroom is made of a special glass that is clear when open and turns opaque when closed. The limestone floor is the same inside and outside, increasing the sense of space and openness. The aesthetic of the scheme is white on white. This apartment is a poetic response to the inherently romantic setting of a forgotten rooftop, providing the owner with a one-off *pied-à-terre*.

Micro-apartments Everyone has seen photographs of the Japanese station hotels that look like stacked washing machines. Each 'room' is reached by a series of ladders and has just enough space for a bed and a television. Other facilities are shared away from the sleeping quarters. The idea is

not new – these 'hotels' are really just dormitories – but there is something worryingly claustrophobic about the images. Yet the idea of finding small spaces in which to stay or live becomes particularly important when considering the problems of inner-city housing. With property prices rising in many cities there has been much demand for flexible studio space. A bold response has been created by young designers Percy Conner who were commissioned to design a micro-apartment to be displayed in the window of Selfridges department store in London. The widespread public interest prompted the architects to design a whole building containing a minimum of 36 micro-flats. From the outside, the façade takes an expressionistic standpoint, in which each apartment is an object animating the street. Some are pushed forwards while others have balconies. Within, they measure only 30 sq m (323 sq ft), demanding design principles

Opposite On first inspection the hotch potch of windows and roofs that makes up this Viennese apartment by EOK Architects looks unfinished, but each element is cleverly designed. the large window next to the kitchen opens up to form a tiny roof terrace. Above Mark Guard's super-minimal apartment on the roof of an old department store in Paris commands spectacular views across the city. Right The interior is simple and uncluttered, making the most of the space available.

the other side of which is the living area and kitchen. A work space can also be shut away from view, leaving enough space for a sofa and dining table. There is little room for clutter and storage, but then the idea is to provide affordable housing for key workers in central locations. Currently the building remains on the drawing board but it cannot be long before a project of this kind is realized.

In central Paris the post office commissioned a building to provide affordable accommodation for its workers, with some apartments for individuals and others for couples. The design, by Phillipe Gazeau, consists of carefully controlled vertical blocks connected by stairs and decks. From the outside the building reads as though it has been vertically split into one third and two thirds. One block is 3.5m (11½ft) wide by 15m (50ft) long and houses studio accommodation while the other is 7.5m (25ft) wide and contains larger apartments. The gap in between serves as the circulation space where simple metal stairs open out on to generous timber-floored balconies, with lightweight balustrades, overlooking the main street. Dark-coloured engineering brick defines the skin, although the main elevations are animated by tall windows and sliding shutters. The apartments themselves are neat and well planned with good-quality fittings, providing a model for welfare homes.

Breaking the mould While the constraints of building homes in urban areas appear problematic and expensive to overcome, it is refreshing to see how many people are prepared to seek out opportunities to experiment and create new responses to our ever-changing urban environments. Even established typologies such as the semi-detached house and the tenement building can provide frameworks for imaginative architectural solutions, the realization of which can only bring vigour and personality to their neighbourhoods. The need to create habitable environments remains a primary concern for all of us and one that connects cities from one side of the globe to the other. There are an infinite number of variations on the theme, which will surely secure the future of the intelligently designed urban house.

that are usually applied to yacht interiors or caravans. Everything must have its place: it should have the ability to fold away, and it must be multifunctional. The plan is not dissimilar to a hotel room. The basic footprint is a rectangle with a lobby where one comes in the front door. To one side is a bedroom pod, really just the size of a double bed, which can be shut off using folding screens, which in turn allow private access to the shower room. The geometry of the bathroom slips to form an angle, on

Left A computer rendering shows a possible solution for dense urban housing by London designers Percy Connor. The concept can be applied to a number of sites with different external languages employing a varied palette of materials. *Opposite* These stylish apartment buildings were designed for post office workers in Paris by Phillipe Gazeau. The timber cladding has a humanizing effect on the city location.

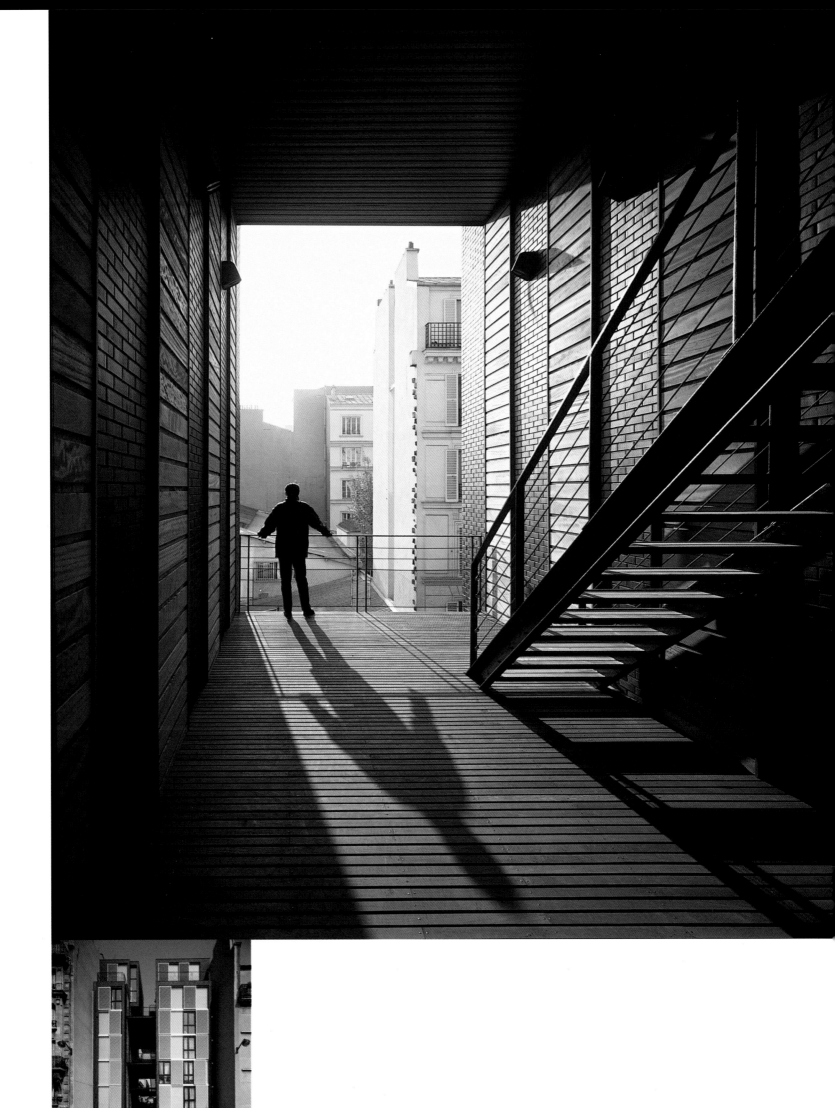

4. Escape Homes

Escape Homes
Nature and Nurture

Nature not artifice

The opposition of city to country is a simplistic one, not least when considering the kinds of homes in which people wish to live. While urbanites might dream of fleeing the metropolitan rat trap to a quiet retreat, new visitors to urban centres may be thrilled and energised by the city. Equally, city dwellers may be appalled at the unsophisticated and slow pace of life in the country, and those not accustomed to the hubbub of the metropolis can find it stressful and dirty. Historically, the countryside has been poor and the work difficult, a situation that in some places remains to this day. Social tension between indigenous dwellers and incomers suggests that there is no such place as Eden and escapism is a relative phenomenon.

Nevertheless many urban dwellers still go in search of a rural retreat, a place of escape to a more peaceful, therapeutic and less pressured existence. Life in the country is perceived as simpler and truer, connecting the individual with nature and the earth. Here, consideration for the practicalities of everyday living can be partially dispensed with and a much more pared down, idealistic way of being can be experienced. The development of information technology has meant that work patterns are now more nomadic and traditional family structures

more flexible. The primary dwelling instincts of man have been challenged by this newfound connectivity. It is a significant factor contributing to the phenomenon of escapism and the trend to migrate towards cities may even be in the process of reversing, as it is now possible to stay in touch through virtual communities and networks. Meanwhile, we search for a more centred, stable environment which has a closer relationship with natural cycles as an antidote to such change. For some this may be a permanent home, for others a place for weekends or vacations may suffice.

Other, less tangible issues can explain the attraction of the countryside. Not least is the fact that the city is increasingly understood as a 'non-place', a term suggesting alienation and a lack of cohesion, whereas a particular part of the countryside may be more easily comprehended as having a unique identity. This might be a single view, the edge of a river or the shade of a tree; the location of a building gathers its own meanings from

its relationship to nature and the seasons. In previous centuries, nature was taken to be a representation of the 'divine', but the search today is for an altogether more empirical form of spirituality. In his significant book *Genius Loci* (1979), Christian Norberg-Schulz explores the notion of 'dwelling' alongside an understanding of 'being'. He concludes that in our rational, information-based culture, it is increasingly difficult to 'dwell poetically' and hence our lives feel ever more meaningless. This philosophical stance may appear remote and difficult, yet it does access the central question: why does it matter where and how we live? There has to be some sense of purpose in building a house and making a home, wherever it is, and it is not just a question of style.

As the trend for alternative lifestyles is peddled by the media and per capita income rises, for many the idea of commissioning a new house is no longer a dream and the search for rural sanctuaries has recently produced a number of poetic and

Above Poking its head above an oak forest, the 25m (80ft) Tower House at Fayetteville, Arkansas, United States, is both a poetic sanctuary and a look-out post from which to commune with the natural world.

thoughtful new homes, one-off experiments in house building that demonstrate the continued desire to create new domestic contexts that frame and connect with the landscape. Architecture has the ability to set up a dialogue between nature and the manmade, expressing both the attitudes of the owner and of the times.

New contexts

Rural domestic architecture has developed over long periods of time and as such reflects the continuity of history. The desire to preserve the countryside and its vernacular architecture, though, can be nostalgic and devolutionary but, at its best, makes relevant old structures and dwellings. There still exists a prejudice that modern buildings and homes are inappropriate in rural settings but those designed with an awareness of context and a sensitivity to local traditions can bring a new beauty and sense of place to their locales.

The building of a new wing on to a traditional German farmhouse goes a long way towards proving that old and new can sit together respectfully. Architect Christoph Mäckler was invited to add a wing on to an ancient winery set on the banks of Lake Constance in Germany. The existing sixteenth-century building was no longer used to produce wine and had become a protected structure. The owners' brief called for additional accommodation as the ground floor had become so damp as to be uninhabitable. The solution was to propose a separate building, just 3.7m (12ft) wide by 18m (60ft) deep, which was connected to the winery by a glazed bridge at first-floor level.

The tapered concrete structure appears to be floating, as the underside cantilevers well past a single supporting column, which can be seen as a homage to Modernism. On the other side, from the lake aspect, a concrete box serves to anchor the building and acts as the communal space and kitchen, while the construction above contains four bedrooms and a bathroom. The connections between the slab and the base are articulated by four curious compressed elements which appear to be under stress as they hold up the whole building. The side elevation of the new building reveals a carefully composed canvas: the bathroom is expressed as a raw concrete box protruding from a white flat plane and small square slot windows give specific views on to the surrounding countryside from within the bedrooms.

The concrete is also expressed within the building but the detailing here is very fine: there is a timber lining to the concrete wall and a playful chequerboard floor in the bathroom. The staircase is a wafer-thin, folded concrete slab which cantilevers from the external wall and leads to the bedrooms which are flooded with light. Here the windows are articulated as a Bauhaus composition, with heavy, dark glazing bars interrupted by the odd solid panel of red or yellow.

This project can be read as an essay that compares and contrasts the architectural values of the past with the gymnastic possibilities of today. It does not try to subvert or change the existing conditions; instead the extension acts as a visual counterpoint to the massive, cracked façade of the old building. While the farmhouse is solid and formal, with square shuttered windows and stone lintels, the new building is lean, elegant and open. The sense of privacy that dominates the traditional house is reversed in the new building, where transparency and light make it possible to see deep inside. Only the family room and kitchen remain semi-submerged, as though buried in the earth itself, making a symbolic connection with primeval forms of shelter and ancient domestic ritual.

Man and nature The dialogue between a building and its setting is critical if it is to appear harmonious and anchored. For example, a house in Lège in the South of France by architects Lacton and Vassal is suspended among trees with a view over water to the horizon. The house is an aluminium box held up on metal columns and in order to preserve the 'as found' nature of the site, the trunks of the trees penetrate the structure creating another, metaphorical supporting system. They exit the roof through square rooflights which have expanding joints around the trunks to allow for movement. The interior provides a contrast between the industrial galvanized steel columns, the polished concrete floor and the rough bark of the tree trunks. A terrace is cantilevered out from the living space which is connected to the ground by a spiral staircase, the only way in and out of the house. Upstairs there are four small bedrooms and two bathrooms arranged across the back of the plan, opening into the main living area. This highly specialized 'tree house' gives the owners a unique sense of occupation. It is unusual to live in the trees alongside the birds, literally without having a foot on the ground. The fact that the trees are actually

growing through the house creates a living dialogue between the structure and nature, highlighting the differences between the manmade steels and the gnarled trunks of the trees.

Situated in a more tamed natural environment, a small shack designed by Niall Mclaughlin for a photographer is a characterful, insect-like structure. It is set on the side of a small manmade pond in an area that used to be a USAF reconnaissance base in England. When first viewed it is easy to imagine that this building is a winged creature with a life of its own, hovering next to the edge of a pool, ready to dart off in an instant; locals call it the 'dragonfly'. According to the architect, the design also makes references to reconnaissance aircraft, reflecting the history of the site. The building houses a studio, a sleeping space and a sauna. It had an incredibly low budget owing to the way the building was procured. There were no drawings of the building as such; instead a series of scale models was made and these were interpreted on site. This clear departure from normal architectural process shows a much tighter bond of trust between the designer and the builder/maker.

The shack consists of a collection of materials that have been woven and spliced together in an organic way; in one sense it is a patchwork, in another an Airfix kit. The roof is a series of scales made from plywood, fibreglass and polycarbonate held in place by steel rods. As the roof angles up a tiny glass box pops up bringing light down into the space below. The walls are constructed from rendered blocks and different-shaped windows have been cut out of them, reading as a collection of framed still-life photographs from within. A series of decks allows the inhabitants to float above the water and enjoy the view. The architect was interested in the way light could be reflected and refracted as it entered the building and the white walls are drenched in sunlight filtered through perforated mesh screens. This effect is enhanced by carefully placed bottles and other glass objects which refract the light, casting their colour on to the floor and the walls. The building has also been made to weather well, changing its appearance over time. The metal roofing sheets have begun to turn green,

streaks are appearing around the rivets and deposits are left in the earth. The timber has dulled down and plants have begun to envelope the edges, making the building appear to meld with its natural setting.

Environment matters

Climate plays a big part in the way we inhabit our constructed worlds. In the cold of winter the hearth acts as a cosy centre to the home, a place around which to congregate, while in summer the outdoor terrace becomes a room in its own right, sheltered from the daytime sun by plants or awnings, at night serving as a cool place to eat and drink. Architecture can temper natural climatic conditions, blurring the boundary between indoors and outdoors. Developments in glass technology mean that larger than ever sheets of double-glazed material can be manufactured to create homes that are transparent and light, with a real sense of openness to the elements. In remote rural settings it is more feasible to utilize huge expanses of glass without worrying about privacy. Low emissivity glass allows in light but not heat, making it possible to regulate indoor temperature in a way that is energy efficient and kind to the environment.

In wild and beautiful settings, the need to design buildings that are not profligate with energy and natural resources takes on a particular relevance. Heating and air-conditioning systems require power, cost money and waste non-renewable resources, and their own production is essentially damaging to the environment. It is far better, where possible, to design systems that can respond to their own micro-climates; to have glass panels or windows that open to promote natural circulation, and walls and roofs that are well insulated for warmth in winter and coolness in summer. Heating can be kept to a minimum if a combined heating and recycled energy unit is specified, with a heat-recovery system. Likewise, solar panels can either supplement the household energy supply or provide power for the entire building. The materials used in construction are also a consideration. Building with wood from sustainable sources, local or recycled materials is now seen as a responsible choice as well as rooting the architecture within its local environment.

Opposite This Australian beach house by Nik Karalis is an elegant essay in simple Modernist design, favouring simplicity of structure, maximum glazing and open-plan living. *Right* Sam Mockbee's Bryant House in Hale County, Alabama, United States, is a collage of natural and recycled materials that have been put together to form a simple but artful dwelling. The design encompasses a generous front porch and reflects the regional architecture.

Left and opposite **This sophisticated eco-house on the uninhabited Skorvon Island off Finland was designed by London-based architect Seth Stein using the latest technology. The wooden house was entirely prefabricated and assembled in situ over two summers. It is powered by solar panels attached to the curved roof.**

Opposite *This elemental timber-clad box was designed by Henning Larsen to be a retreat and studio for an artist couple in Vejby, Zealand, Denmark. The larch cladding will eventually turn grey, causing the building to meld with the wooded landscape.*

Above *The interior is clad in native birch-ply panels; its zen-like simplicity is a perfect place for escape and contemplation.*

Contemporary vernacular

Wherever one goes in the world it is easy to spot groups of agricultural buildings and small cottages scattered about the countryside that appear to have grown up out of the landscape surrounding them. They appear somehow natural and grounded. As the process of industrialization changes the face of the countryside, however, they are vacated or become disused and are perfect for rediscovery by new owners. In a rural context, converting an existing building is a much easier route to making a new home than starting from scratch. This approach, which deals with an understanding of locality and the everyday aspects of vernacular architecture, begins to connect the past to the present, materials to landscape, and helps to create homes that have a sense of place. There remain those who feel that to copy examples of architecture from another age is unacceptable. Yet a growing body of architects and designers maintain that vernacular architecture is born out of a thoughtful way of making and constructing rather than simply refining a style.

Left The barn-like design of the Marshall House by Dow Jones Architects is an interpretation of the traditional local architecture. It has a timeless quality and yet manages to be quietly subversive at the same time. *Opposite* The rear elevation of Whithurst Park Cottage in Sussex, England, designed by James Gorst, displays a formal though asymmetric composition reminiscent of Robert Venturi's house for his mother built 40 years earlier (see p.36). It is described by the architect as a 'contemporary barn'.

The Marshall House in rural Suffolk, England, is a prime example of this methodology. The form of the house, designed by Dow Jones Architects, is similar to those of local barns. It is built with a red brick base and clad in black timber weatherboarding. The roof is pitched and covered with red clay tiles; on the short elevation a chimney breast is expressed as a vertical brick appendage. It is the wilful arrangement of the windows that begins to suggest that the building is not simply a barn. A large, glazed, floor-to-ceiling window on the ground floor signifies the main living space, while a series of different-shaped windows creates a balanced but not symmetrical composition on the two long façades. The arrangement of rooms is very simple: there is a large living room, a kitchen and a large cloakroom on the ground floor and a timber-clad staircase leads upstairs to three bedrooms and a bathroom. On closer inspection, the arrangement is not as normal as it seems at first. The living space is barn-like, but with a semi-enclosed stair on an axis with the fireplace, while behind the stair is the unusually

generous cloakroom. The kitchen is also large, fitted out with a minimum of built-in equipment. Upstairs there is one communal bathroom for three bedrooms and a capacious landing. These inflections on the plan suggest a rejection of en suite facilities and fitted details; the house is a simple container for the inhabitants to bring in their own possessions. This allows it to appear both traditional and modern at the same time.

The use of materials such as brick and Douglas fir lend a familiarity and warmth to the interior, without being nostalgic in their references. The brick floor inside is a grid, turning up the wall as a deep skirting, expressing the form of construction (it is also the external plinth); on the end wall it wraps up the wall to form the hearth and chimney breast. The ceiling and some special walls are clad in pale wood (see p.45). By night the windows of the barn glow in a slightly eerie way. There is something about the austerity of the spaces that suggests a Calvinist way of life, even that of the millennarist sect the Shakers, who owned all their property in common.

Above This remote summer house belonging to two architects in Denmark is another barn-like structure with a low pitched roof; the large picture window of the living area, however, indicates that it is a special building. Within, the materials have been carefully edited, lending the interior a polished edge.

A different type of experiment in timber building can be found in a tiny Danish village near Aarhus, where a modest timber house, designed by the architect owners Dombernowsky and Christensen, represents an alternative to the kit houses often chosen by local people for their summer homes. The duo claim that there is no tradition of timber houses in Denmark and that the house owes more to Swedish or Norwegian examples. That said it does appear to be in the mould of surrounding agricultural buildings and in plan it makes reference to the Danish long house.

The overall form is once again barn-like, though here a double-height window suggests a contemporary modernist habitation. The exterior is clad in oiled Siberian larch with an overhanging pitched roof finished in zinc. The arrangement of rooms was specifically designed for the architect's family: the ground floor is shared by a large living/kitchen area with two bedrooms and a bathroom for the children; an open stair leads up to a living room, a master bedroom and a small guest room. The ground-floor finish is polished concrete with natural timber cladding wrapping up walls and ceilings. Upstairs the walls are simply painted white with a natural timber floor. This home is a slicker and more spatially complex building than the Marshall House and seems to enjoy playing architectural games. The planning here incorporates clever multifunctional details and has a generally more bespoke interior. The result is a charming essay in collaging modern materials with simple architectural forms.

In domestic architecture the relationship between the form of a building and its function has, for a long time, been a strong generating force, but it

is unusual to see the design of a rural house that uses this as the literal point of departure. Set into the rolling hills and woods of the Calamuchita Valley in Argentina, and far away from the busy metropolitan life of Cordoba, is a modest but clever holiday home. The diagram for this house is very different from the norm: it is essentially a glazed box with four stone turrets at each corner and on plan it resembles a small fortress. It is the collision of an ancient, almost primitive, stone-wall architecture with one that is slick and modern. The grey sandstone on the outside is laid in a traditional way similar to that of dry-stone walling and serves to highlight the building's solidity and link it to a vernacular past. Windows are small, square, deep punctures that let in a minimal amount of light to the service spaces, keeping them well insulated and cool. Full-height glass doors slide open, connecting the main space with the terrace outside. When not in use another layer of folding cedar panels closes the house off. A final layer of insect screens means that the doors can be left open at night, cooling the rooms by natural ventilation. The front door is on one side of a glass triangular bay window – where it acts as a marker – and on an axis with the hearth.

The internal arrangement is simple enough: the main space is the living room which includes open-plan sleeping areas and a dining table, while the kitchen, laundry, bathroom and storage areas are each enclosed in their own stone surrounds. These cave-like interiors work in the opposite way to the main space; they are enclosed, private and rustic. While only ever a weekend residence, this house does communicate an essential interpretation of what constitutes a home, having both the open glass room as well as intimate corners and tucked-away rooms.

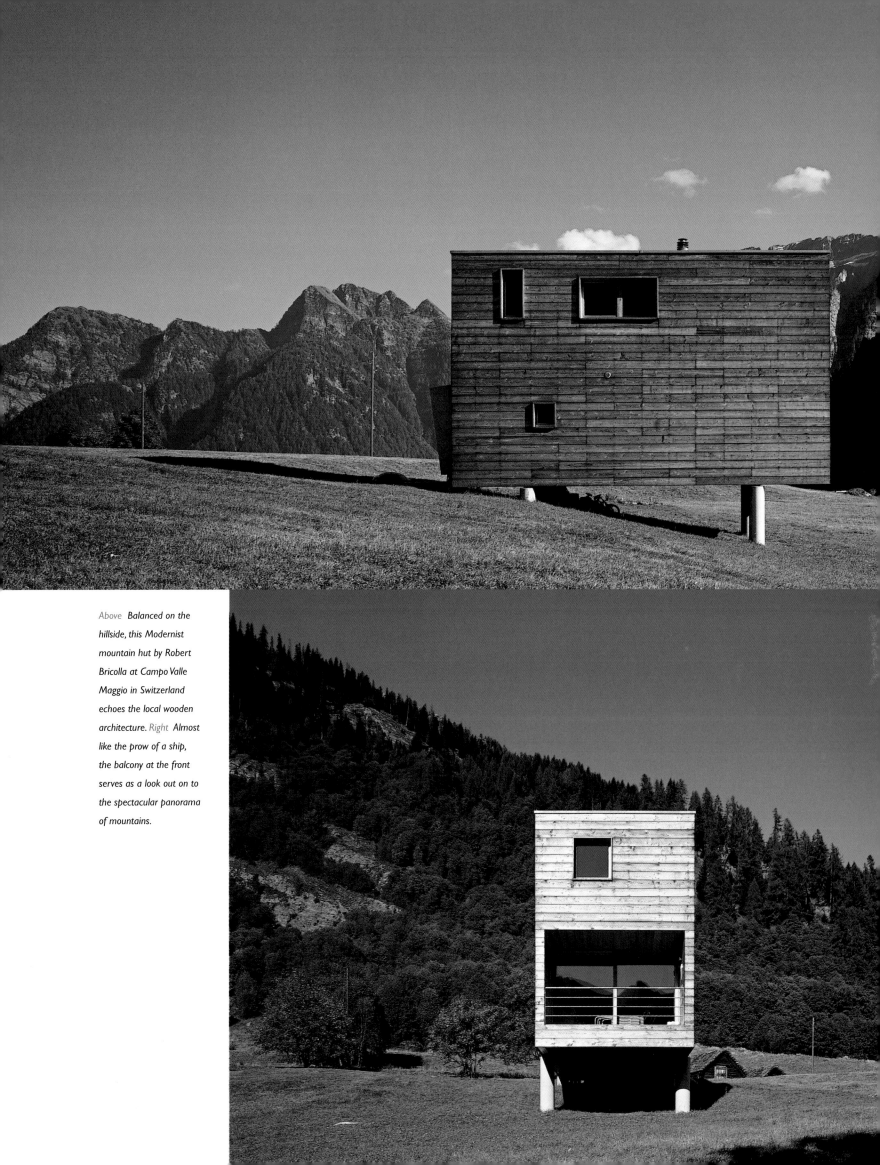

Above Balanced on the hillside, this Modernist mountain hut by Robert Bricolla at Campo Valle Maggio in Switzerland echoes the local wooden architecture. *Right* Almost like the prow of a ship, the balcony at the front serves as a look out on to the spectacular panorama of mountains.

Splendid isolation The search for isolation can be the driving force behind commissioning a house set in the middle of nature, disconnected from the infrastructure of manmade environments. This romantic ideal is often hard to find in practice. When a rare opportunity to build in this kind of location is found, the question of buildability must be considered. Often a prefabricated solution is appropriate. When building the Malator House on the remote Pembrokeshire coast in Wales, the architects Future Systems had to consider how to make a hi-tech underground home on the edge of a cliff. The clients had stayed in an old army hut on the site for a number of years before deciding they wanted a brand new home. The radical proposal for a semi-buried dwelling caught their imagination as it would restore the site to a green field and at the same time offer a completely contemporary living environment. Construction involved digging out tons

of earth and sinking the structural shell, made of waterproof marine ply, which was to become the container for living in. This was then covered in soil and laid with turf, camouflaging the building in the landscape. Another benefit of the thick roof is its insulating properties, keeping the heat inside during winter and allowing the space to stay cool in summer. The main façade is a fully glazed opening with doors and portholes to assist in the ventilation. The living area is behind the glass wall, while the bedrooms and bathrooms are arranged on either side. The bright yellow kitchen and glossy white ceiling reflect the daylight, giving a permanent glow of sunshine, making the overall conceit more spacecraft than cave.

Architect Marlon Blackwell has created a sanctuary way above ground-level at Fayetteville, Arkansas, in the United States. His client, the owner of the 22.6 hectare (56 acre) forest site, tells an

endearing story about his grandfather building him a tree house which he was forced to abandon at the age of six when his parents moved away. Years later he found a site near his family home which he felt would be suitable for building a retreat. The result is an extraordinary 25m (80ft) tower poking up above the tree canopy. The idea of a tree house was transformed into a single free-standing structure when it was found that the local trees were not robust enough to support the scale of project envisaged. The tower's design takes its cue from local vernacular buildings. The structure is made of steel tubes and is wrapped in white steel, though a wedge, which reaches up to 15m (50ft), is clad in vertical natural-oak lattice to create a conversation between the building and the surrounding trees. There is a band of windows all the way around the building towards the top, while above a more random series of openings suggests

a further place of inhabitation. Inside a metal stair rises above the tree tops to reach the first room, which is used for living and sleeping. The room is dominated by the horizontal window and the 360-degree panorama. A staircase that pulls down from the ceiling provides the final ascent to the 'sky court' on the roof. This open-air room is enclosed though there are openings on all four sides to frame particular views.

In some ways the building is a folly; it did not have to be so tall and as such is an indulgence. Yet it remains a delightful piece of patronage and a personal monument. It is used by the owner as a place to relax and occasionally work, but it has also been hijacked by the local school as a destination for a day out. This kind of building testifies to the power of architectural iconography. It can be seen from far off and has brought character and particularity to this neighbourhood.

The benign identity of the Tower House has meant that its history has been absorbed into local folklore; the story of the owner and his grandfather has spread among the community. In a final episode, the owner tells how his 88-year-old grandfather came to visit the new tree house and insisted on climbing all the way up himself, a moment his grandson will always remember.

At the age of 70, in 1937, the architect Frank Lloyd Wright began building his winter architecture school, Taliesin West, in the Arizona desert. His vision was to create a place of learning away from the sprawl of Phoenix. He chose a site set among the red sandy rocks and saguaro cacti and began constructing a home for himself, an office where students would learn as apprentices and a performance space. His own house was constructed of stone, cement, canvas and timber and appeared to grow out of the desert landscape. The angled, pitched roofs were held in place by externally expressed steel beams and protected the living spaces from the harsh sunlight. The students were expected to learn about design and construction by actually building their own living quarters. They were given small plots of land and charged with designing a hut for three or four people which then had to be built. They also became involved in building the main school and were given tough assignments, such as casting concrete walls from desert rocks, which would be condemned and demolished if Wright felt they were not up to scratch. Their small buildings varied greatly in character; while some were simple shelters using only canvas, others were complex architectural compositions using the same materials as Wright's own house. Wright became distraught when the authorities began erecting pylons in his particular piece of wilderness, even threatening to leave Taliesin.

In a similar location in Tucson, Arizona, architect Rick Joy has recently constructed a new, single-storey house surrounded by desert and cacti. It has an inverted pitched roof, known as a butterfly roof, covered in pre-rusted corrugated metal sheeting and supported by massive cast-concrete walls which appear to be the same outside and in. Although it is a very solid building the plan has been designed as a pinwheel, where the front door is the centre of a series of rooms and spaces that are arranged off it. The living space is anchored by a block of concrete which contains the fireplaces, one inside and the other outside on a terrace that is sheltered by part of the overhanging roof. The timber shuttering for the concrete walls, which holds the wet concrete in place as it sets, was made in short lengths which left their rough imprint on the walls once the timber had been removed. The result is an imprint of timber that acts as a memory of the natural material which has since been removed, and the concrete has the appearance of a fossilized wall. Inside, the language of rough concrete walls is offset by a polished concrete floor, white plastered ceiling and glass-clad bathrooms. The views framed by the large windows are of expanses of the rugged desert landscape, while within there exists a highly tuned contemporary setting.

At the water's edge

Houses sited next to the sea inhabit some of the world's most romantic locations with views of sandy beaches, windswept coastlines and golden sunsets. There are many precedents for buildings at the water's edge such as fisherman's cottages, sheds for boats, beach huts and shacks of all kinds. Traditionally many of these are timber constructions embedded in rocky foundations which need to be maintained annually to ensure structural stability and waterproofing. For the Modernists, building by the sea presented the possibility of designing new types of houses that drew their references from the streamlined ocean liners of the industrial age. Today there is a more eclectic response to seaside architecture ranging from rock star villas isolated on the coast of Malibu in California to the myriad balconied apartments lining the Mediterranean. Whatever the response, the iconic relationship between the sea and the land continues to be a great inspiration to architects and their clients.

In East Hampton, New York, architect Preston T Phillips has built a neat beach house on a newly constructed pier. The two hectare (five acre) site was purchased by the owners so that they could find the seclusion and proximity to the ocean that

they were looking for. The cost of the house was only a fraction of that of the land. From a distance the building has two distinct parts: a gazebo temple surrounded by railings and a collection of white accommodation boxes on the other end of the mini pier. The massing of the buildings is simple, comprising a glazed space with butterfly roofs sandwiched between two flat-roofed boxes. They are all clad in pre-painted metal siding, a material more commonly used for industrial or agricultural buildings. The interior is simple and understated, with a galley kitchen next to the main living space, a bathroom and a bedroom. The wall dividing sleeping and living areas contains a double-sided fireplace. The house was designed to be opened up and for the decks to be inhabited. An outside shower suggests a casual and relaxed lifestyle which is very different from the air-conditioned mansions farther up the beach. At 93 sq m (1,000 sq ft) the house is the size of a traditional two-bed apartment. Here, however, it becomes an object on the beach.

A classic response to a secluded beach setting is found in the Gough House by Craig Rosevear which is set into the sand dunes that overlook Storm Bay in Hobart, Tasmania. Both the client and the architect were interested in using structure in an inventive and expressive way and the idea of a 'trussed bridge' emerged. The building was designed to sit on a small timber-clad base, containing a bathroom and a store, thus minimizing the environmental impact. The body of the house cantilevers over the base along its length, lending a precarious sense of balance. It also means that the views are uninterrupted.

On arrival at the house the visitor must walk the last 50m (165ft) up and over a sand dune before arriving at the lower level; once inside the main living space on the upper floor, the view opens up. A core containing the bathroom and kitchen accommodation divides the sleeping area from the rest of the house. The ethos of the design is essentially minimal, apart from the structure which is

Above Viewed from the beach the Gough House, in Hobart, Tasmania, hovers above the sand dunes. The cantilevered structure is daring, though certainly not minimal, providing 360-degree views of the surrounding seascape.
Opposite The distorted geometry of the Cape Schnack House near Melbourne, Australia, creates an arresting, quirky retreat. Within the layout is simple, revealing panoramas of the sea which can be shut off using external blinds.

visible on the outside. The steel frame was prefabricated and assembled on site due to the remoteness of the location. At a technical level, it is surprising to find an exposed steel frame bolted in place, as it is open to the elements and the chance of corrosion is high. The architect argues, however, that because every joint is visible any deterioration can be spotted and treated. An additional advantage of following this route was the opportunity to avoid expensive factory finishing.

Inside, the sliding frame doors are simple, perhaps slightly crude, only because the setting itself demands an uninterrupted view, which can be achieved by sitting on the balcony projection with its glass balustrade. There is little sense of enclosure, as even the bedroom area has no curtains. The bed itself is part of the fabric of the building, a cantilevered steel platform connected to the main structure which can flex in strong winds, transmitting the weather conditions outside to those within, who are snug in bed. This connection

to natural forces demonstrates a sensitivity not immediately obvious from the outside. It is clear that the house owes something to the tradition of Modernism, in particular the glass houses of Mies van der Rohe and Australian architect Glenn Murcutt. This is not to say, however, that it does not posses its own power and charm. What it demonstrates is our ongoing seduction by the idea of the glass box which in this case acts as an elevated lookout post over the horizon. The house stands as a monument to modernity and the iconic juxtaposition of formal manmade objects and untamed natural surroundings.

A similarly bold structural idea generated the form of the Cape Schnack House. Built by Denton Corker Marshall Architects, it sits like a dark shard projecting from a rocky outcrop overlooking the Mornington Peninsula, which is south of Melbourne in Australia. The compressed-cement sheet cladding wraps around the two long sides and roof at an angle, giving the building a twisted dynamic. It is less

open than the Gough House, with windows at both ends and a long horizontal slot creating views from the living area along the long side, which can be softened by lowering external blinds. The dark painted surface of the exterior absorbs the light, emphasizing the mass of the building.

Within, a series of cubes, not reaching the angled ceiling, hold the functional areas of the home. One is clad in timber and contains the bathroom, and separates living from sleeping areas, while another is a kitchen pod. That such elements are separated relates more to the idea of outdoor living or camping than to traditional rooms. The play between forms is wilful and yet not overly obtrusive. The floor is polished concrete, extending through the glass door to an outside terrace. Again there is a reference to the master architect Mies van der Rohe and the tradition of Modernism is seen here in the deliberate use of cruciform steel columns which hold up the roof in front of the long window. The fireplace is also conceived as an element and is contained within a sheet of galvanized steel. It is identified on the outside by a maverick chimney jutting out at an angle to the main façade. Below there are two further guest rooms with a bathroom and utility space housed in a block that employs a different geometry to the one above. A concrete stair at this level is enclosed by a glass envelope and is the main way into the house.

From some angles this house is monolithic, less of a home and more of a sculptural form. This raises questions about its assumed identity: does a house have to look like a house or can it be open to interpretation by the passer-by? The careful juxtaposition of materials and form reinforces the sense of it as a specially crafted object. Once again the adjacency of the manmade object to the tea trees and the view of the ocean serves to emphasize the uniqueness of the setting. In some ways the lifestyle that is hinted at remains urbane – the spaces are generous and all the comforts of home have been provided – as though the building could fall anywhere, so long as there was a great view. This may be construed as a criticism, yet there is no reason why remoteness should always be linked to the desire to get back to a rustic way of life; it is good to find progressive ideas making their way out of the urban environment to somewhere more remote and wild.

On shorelines with more severe climates the design must accommodate a wider variety of conditions. One such example is a long narrow house in Nova Scotia that juts out on a spit of land surrounded by water on three sides. This landmark house, designed by Brian MacKay-Lyons Architecture for a young family, has a shed-like appearance with façades made of corrugated galvanized metal. The angled roof is highest at the water's edge to protect

the house from the prevailing westerly winds. Windows have been carefully set into the façade in a knowingly compositional way. A large opening towards the back of the house reads like a sliding barn door but leads to the garage and courtyard, which serve as the entrance to the house, and a shaded verandah. This protected area provides shelter and a place to play. A large piece of rock is left in one corner, perhaps as a reminder of the solidity and timelessness of nature. Light is filtered through the timber roof structure, casting a complex pattern of shadows on the ground. The arrangement within is linear and unobstructed; the entrance flows into the kitchen, which in turn opens up into the living area. The corner window of the living area is double height, acting as a marker or beacon at night. A staircase leads up to the mezzanine and the master bedroom or down to the basement and three further bedrooms. It is a spacious and generous living environment, which uses a vernacular agricultural form to make a link between domestic life and the sheds used by the fishing industry that supports these remote communities. The design is clunky in some respects, yet has a refreshing honesty.

On the edge of Espoo in Finland Jyrki Tasa has designed a quirky, experimental home. The site is a high rock that offers a westerly view of the sea and sunsets; the eastern side protected from the winds

by a curved wall. From the outside the house is a collage of materials and forms: a flat, curved wooden roof is seemingly propped up like a canopy by angled stakes that are anchored to the ground; walls are clad in timber, save for a concrete tower. To get to the house, the visitor must first cross a metal bridge over a pool before arriving at the front door which is a long sliver of glass. The entrance hall and stair are the hub of all circulation. The stair itself is a three-storey plywood structure suspended from the ceiling by steel cables. Tall windows offer spectacular views out towards the sea. The tower contains three chimneys and two fireplaces that open out to an indoor swimming pool and living room.

The client is a single male who wanted enough room to entertain guests, so the living spaces are relatively large compared to the bedrooms. Internally, many of the walls are clad in pine plywood and, with the cherrywood floor, this creates a rich and comforting experience for the visitor and lends an authentically Scandinavian flavour to the spaces. The gymnastics of the staircase coupled with the compositional games that are played by the architecture have resulted in a building that is part house, part shed and part architectural model. Externally, it is difficult to understand the scale of the tall building owing to the fact that the setting itself is scaleless – miles of ocean and huge skies.

Natural connection The common theme of all these approaches to building houses away from defined centres of inhabitation is the desire to create personal environments which are enhanced by a sense of place. Whether perched on a cliff or embedded in a forest, these homes dissolve the boundaries between inside and outside, allowing for a more fundamental way of living that is responsive to the seasons and the elements. This emancipation creates a synergy between nature and dwelling that is seldom found in cities and towns.

The notion of an 'escape' home is something deeply personal. For many the combination of a particular setting and architectural expression makes for a unique experience that cannot be found anywhere else.

Left In Jyrki Tasa's Into House at Espoo in Finland, vast glazed walls provide magnificent views of the coastline and flood the interior with light.
Below left The curved wall of the side and rear aspects protects the house from the prevailing winds.
Opposite The owners of these two new houses in rural France by Eric Gouesnard have created their own natural idyll: the garden has been planned as a meadow reached via timber boardwalks, baked in the sun.

5. Mass Housing

Mass Housing
New Patterns of Development

Urban infrastructure

In the urbanized setting of Europe and America most people will have grown up in houses just like the one next door; in suburbs, apartment blocks and housing complexes. The global need to construct mass housing was born out of the nineteenth-century population explosion and the results can be surprisingly similar across national boundaries. The Victorian streets of Sydney resemble those in London and the same types of apartment blocks in Berlin can also be found in Paris or Vienna, or indeed in most major European cities.

In many ways patterns of house building have defined the characters of the towns and cities we know today. Each has its own story to tell, a history that is retained in its buildings and urban topographies. People often talk about the 'grain' of a city, referring to the density and texture of its streets and buildings. Making cities has been a sedimentary process: the centres of most historic cities consist of layers, built up over time, with the important buildings such as banks, offices, churches and civic headquarters forming a core. Often only the wealthy can afford to live near these central locations, although in the past they were not so obviously desirable, with their primitive sewerage and open drains. In contrast to cosmopolitan city

centres, the urban sprawl of any large city presents an unbelievable amount of woefully inadequate housing, with ugly stained façades, collapsing infrastructure and unloved balconies. Yet they were all once new.

Where there is no historic centre as reference point, planners and architects face considerable challenges when creating new communities from scratch. Many prospective inhabitants of new developments may claim to want traditional types of home. This nostalgia can be seen as a reaction to globalization, fulfilling a need for security, privacy and enclosure. In the book *Strangely Familiar* (1996), the cultural commentator Doreen Massey proposes that the effect of globalization has been to diminish our understanding of the relationship between society and space. The flow of information now made available through the internet and mobile telecommunications is invisible and unspatial, as

opposed to the physical communications networks with which we are more familiar. In the space of the home, new models are required to accommodate the interface with this world. For instance, the traditional use of the bedroom as a child's playroom may not facilitate a computer connection, whereas the study, often a private room, may be the only room with a computer and so must become multi-functional. The presence of boundaries and mono-functional spaces, therefore, has to be addressed if house design is to reflect current models of domesticity. The single home must cater for the needs of a few, which is complex enough, but mass housing has to make a place for many individuals, offering flexibility and richness within an urban setting. Many of the most respected new housing projects do not try to ape the past; rather they attempt to embrace and reflect the spirit of the present. The examples in this section aim to show

Above The roofscape of Manhattan, New York, is a picturesque jumble of old and new; conical water towers on top of historic brick buildings create a silhouette in front of the shiny façades of newer buildings. In high-rise cities people live and work on top of each other, often losing all sense of the street life below.

how new solutions and contemporary forms allow a complex and varied pattern of inhabitation which may be individually customized without compromising the overall identity of the scheme.

Edges, streets and objects
In the 1950s and 1960s belief in the theories of the social sciences was reflected in much architecture of the period: the design of buildings was based on standardized patterns of social behaviour. There was a whole school of thought, in the socialist mould, that sought to empower the masses through collectivization, which sometimes led to the suppression of individual expression in favour of that of the State. In addition, mass production promoted a clunky, repetitive aesthetic. The generation of new housing was reduced to the production of objects – towers, terraces, blocks and slabs – with none of the detailed sensitivity required when creating the fabric of an inhabited space.

Another mistake of much post-war social housing was its siting: cold objects set in desolate landscapes. Neither urban nor suburban, many were led to call these projects 'no place'. The treatment of the edge or boundary of a group of houses is critical to its reading within a city, but the actual ownership of these in-between areas can be problematic. The term 'defensible space' has come to define private space that is adjacent to the public realm, but the boundaries may blur if streets are pedestrian throughways or there are common front gardens. One only has to stray into an unfamiliar residential housing estate to feel unease when the territory feels neither public nor private. What was conceived of as a passage becomes a dangerous alley; a pocket park becomes a menacing meeting place. Architects' drawings often tell an idealized story – children playing, planted borders with the sun shining – thus ignoring other, less desirable inhabitations. The question is, who really owns these spaces, manages them and protects them? As a response to criticisms of seemingly misplaced architectural heroics, many recent housing projects have sought to create communities and spaces that relate to their occupants as well as seeking to construct dwellings that are flexible and appropriate to people's needs.

New urban alternatives An austere, provocative response to the question of the street can be found in some publicly assisted housing in Ghent, Belgium, by Neutelings Riedijk Architecten. Two strips of buildings are made up of 15 blocks, each containing eight to ten homes. Entry to the houses is from a central courtyard and there is gallery access to the apartments. The buildings themselves are monolithic, though broken down by the massing that articulates smaller, house-size blocks at the upper level; all are clad in strips of cedar which will dull down to a grey colour over time. The street façade is a long screen punctured by double-height vertical slots behind which are the access route and small individual front gardens. The decision to block the view out on to the street could be seen as perverse, but in practice the screen appears to create both a sheltered and charming micro-climate for the residents and an intriguing sculptural perspective along the street.

Although this is high-density housing, there is a sense of peace and tranquillity about the common

parts not usually associated with such an urban location. The design succeeds in creating a strong edge to an ordinary street as well as a sophisticated series of layers, courtyards and gardens behind. There is little obvious connection with the historic architecture of the city, yet it respects the line of the street and stands out in contrast to the surrounding buildings without shouting about it.

A very different urban typology has been explored by Walter Menteth Architects in eight flats in Battersea, close to the Thames in London. Here there was no formal streetscape to address so the idea of the villa – a free-standing house in a garden – was employed. The flats are massed into one 'villa' surrounded by a garden wall which is made of gabions. The homes were specifically designed for single homeless people and families in need, therefore a sense of boundary and community was critical to the resolution of the project. The simple form of the building is a canny response to the minimal budget. The block is made of concrete clad in a high-performance thermal render and has

a high parapet concealing a sloping roof behind. The language of the openings is very precise: square windows are set flush with the render except at the corners, where a window is expressed as a hinged box, proud of the wall plane. The contrast between the textured natural stone of the external wall and the sleek manmade white cube creates a tension between nature and artifice, the rough with the smooth. The garden spaces are punctuated by bright-yellow rubbish bin stores and empty mesh gabions that are filled with planting. Again the abstract but poetic treatment of the garden landscaping demonstrates an acute sensitivity to the design of the setting.

Inside the building the circulation spaces express a strong sense of materiality; the flank walls are simply exposed concrete block with a brightly painted end wall. The staircase is open tread, with fine, vertical-rod railings and handrails. The flats are laid out with all the service elements, such as the kitchens and the bathrooms, grouped in the centre. Though the bathrooms have no natural light, the kitchens are positioned on the hinged corners of the living spaces and so are partly open to the main rooms, recreating a traditional domestic layout, but opened up in a more dynamic way. The

sensitivity towards boundaries both inside and out has resulted in a quietly protective and expressive building which fulfils the needs of its occupants for security and enclosure.

Compare this to a recent social housing scheme in Neu-Ulm, Germany, by GAS-Sahner who are based in Stuttgart. Here, employing similar tactics, 20 dwellings have been built on the site of a former military barracks. Although these homes are surrounded by more green space than the Battersea project, the scheme is still classed as a high-density development. On the outside, a white-rendered box is punctured by horizontal green, yellow and red windows. The potential 'Lego' effect of the primary colours is diluted by the expanse of white walls. The L-shaped plans are the same for all units but are grouped differently to give a subtle sense of individuality. This simple concept allows additional accommodation to be added to the basic plan now or later and in that sense the project is always in flux. Both the Battersea and Neu-Ulm projects succeed in creating a specific sense of place within the context of a tight budget and an architectural language that verges on the minimal. While looking over their shoulder at the past, they remain fresh, inventive and above all modern.

Low rise If the familiar format of the street, with houses on either side, is abandoned then new models of housing have to be considered or successful types, such as the square, appropriated. A good example of the latter approach is found in the latest housing project by Coin Street Community Builders. Situated on London's South Bank, it is a robust example of dense urban housing that maintains a scale appropriate to its location. The scheme, designed by London-based Haworth Tompkins Architects, negotiates its tricky site, which is surrounded on one side by a busy road and on another by office buildings, by drawing on the tradition of the London square. The housing stands around the edge, while the middle of the site becomes a shared space for the residents. The project has 32 houses, 18 maisonettes and nine flats. Their design does not radically try to reinvent the idea of the family house. Each has its own front door, but the identity and uniformity of the block takes precedence over the expression of individual dwellings; in appearance it has a European flavour. The project uses a model appropriate for urban housing and avoids the stylistic problems often associated with attempts at offering individuality. The block itself becomes both an urban landmark as well as a group of houses.

The building's main street façades are clad in brick and its set-back roof storey is clad in zinc. It looks as though an existing warehouse has been converted and extended, and gives the site a sense of narrative. Hidden from view on the roof are solar panels which collect enough energy to provide hot water and some mechanical ventilation to the units. The windows are large, which may sound unremarkable, but this runs against the current predilection for a more rustic idiom, a trend that has resulted in many new houses with tiny, cottage-style openings. There is parking space at street-level and more parking beneath the building – a percentage of these bays are rented out, creating a revenue stream to be used for building maintenance. All the houses possess a small back garden that opens on to the courtyard space.

Within, each home has an open-plan kitchen and living area with bedrooms and bathrooms on

the upper levels. The maisonettes are reached by glazed staircases and have their own balconies which are accessed off an open walkway. From the fourth floor, these homes enjoy views of the river. The design of the internal courtyard elevations features a horizontal collage of timber panels, steel windows and metal balconies. The effect here is more filigree than the outside of the block – the photographs reproduced here were taken before inhabitants started to occupy these external spaces – and it will be interesting to see whether or not the visible detritus of everyday life adds to the

Above Haworth Tompkins Architects have provided generous shared deck access for the rooftop maisonettes at the Coin Street Community project. *Left* The apartments at lower levels have balconies shaded from direct sun by horizontal timber louvres; etched glass screens provide privacy between neighbours. *Opposite above* In the external spaces of Walter Menteth's Battersea project, the harmonious language of white walls, stone and wood creates a tranquil, human environment. *Opposite centre* Menteth's simple white villa contains eight apartments for members of the community in need. *Opposite below* The design for GAS-Sahner's housing in Neu-Ulm, Germany takes a similarly minimal approach.

composition. The public space is divided into four zones, all of which are geared to family life: a playground, a games pitch, a grassed lawn and a hard-landscaped seating area. The setting provides a microcosm of the city; a place open to chance encounters and meetings, which nevertheless belongs to only one group of homes.

New forms It remains one of the quirks of history that modernist sensibilities have only recently become popular again in terms of the mass-housing market. While a minority of innovative developers might speculate on commissioning a design that is inventive, challenging and different, most stick with tried and tested formulas that are often conservative and bland. In other words, the innovation spawned in the 1920s and 1930s that changed the face of the built environment has today been banished. In part this has to do with the fact that for many the pared-down modernist aesthetic became associated with bleak public housing projects for those on low incomes, which were ultimately viewed as failures.

This is particularly well demonstrated in Glasgow in Scotland, a city that has more than its fair share of desolate housing projects, notably the concrete slab blocks known as the Gorbals, which were designed by Basil Spence in the 1960s. When Glasgow was named European City of Culture in 1999, a site was chosen on which to hold a competition for new housing. A masterplan was agreed which brought together a number of architects, including Rick Mather, Ushida Findlay and McKeown Alexander, to design the different blocks. This patchwork model of housing development is more common in Europe and was also used successfully in Fukuoka, Japan, where, during the early 1990s, Rem Koolhaas, Steven Holl, Mark Mac and Christian de Portzamparc designed individual low-rise housing blocks within an agreed framework. The result was an instant neighbourhood, which relied on the juxtaposition of different aesthetics, textures and forms to suggest a hybrid programme which had evolved over time. For the city of Glasgow, this kind of approach to housing was a completely new departure. The site chosen for the

Above left Page and Park's curvy walled housing block, constructed as part of 'Glasgow 1999', breaks down the scale of the building by suggesting a rhythm of rendered walls. Centre left A more sensitive area of the masterplan is found at 50 Graham Square where the old Market Hotel was reconfigured by Richard Murphy Architects. The new design includes 17 one- and two-bedroom apartments. Part of the façade has been removed to create an intriguing courtyard. Below left Another example of new urban housing by Page and Park is found in Edinburgh, Scotland. Here, the architects have conceived the façade as an abstract billboard; a brick base is topped by two stories of accommodation featuring large graphic panels.

competition was in a run-down inner-city zone to the east of the historic city centre. The client was Glasgow City Council who partnered the developers, noting from the outset that they wanted a development that would meet current housing needs while allowing future generations the scope to meet their own.

The detailed language of the architecture on the competition site varies, though thematically it could be described as a hybrid of Modernism. The use of white render and glass contrasts with external timber weatherboarding and utilitarian galvanized steel; the buildings read as crisp, confident but polite statements. The large corporate architectural practice RMJM, who are based in London, developed designs centred around the notion of the villa. Two types were employed: introvert and extrovert. The former comprises four flats and two maisonettes, all containing rooms with roof terraces. The latter is more open-plan, with large windows and a shared roof garden. The introvert apartments are rendered in white while the extrovert flats are clad in horizontal timber boarding. This simple narrative device allows the façades of the buildings to be broken up and offers two complimentary but different aesthetics.

Next door, the housing by Scotland-based architects Elder and Cannon offers a more dynamic and explicitly urban solution. The block itself is seven storeys tall. At ground level there is provision for shops, studios and workshops which are united by a plinth element. Above sits a framed façade of glass and timber with generous doors opening on to shallow balconies, and a curved corner clad in timber. The most striking elements, however, are the apartments on the rooftop which have been rotated and appear to be balancing on top of the building, as though they have just been craned in and are not yet fixed in their correct positions. The effect is arresting and playful, suggesting a building in flux, perhaps not even finished. It also creates a landmark – the building with the twisty top. Designed to be a showcase, inviting comment and criticism in a genuine attempt to capture the public's imagination, Glasgow's collection of 100 new homes offers a lasting vision for the future.

Above Elder and Cannon's contribution to Glasgow's new housing competition is a layered and busy composition topped by a cheeky single unit that appears to be on the move. The overall effect from the street is of an active wall which has numerous devices to break up the monotony of repetition.

Green living A radical housing scheme was recently completed in the South of France on the banks of the River Lez in the centre of Montpellier. Here French architect Edouard François has built a genuinely innovative project thanks to his own passion for 'green' buildings. The 64 flats are arranged in a gentle curve and the building climbs from three to six storeys. While the stony base is solid and unremarkable, the façade of the building was conceived as a growing, living skin. It is made from gabions which are more commonly used to create the edges of motorways. At Montpellier the metal cages are filled with crushed volcanic rock, and also with manure and the seeds of indigenous cacti and figs. An integrated irrigation system keeps the surfaces of the gabion walls damp, thus encouraging the growth of the plants.

This poetic gesture is underlined by a series of timber-clad, open-roofed pavilions hoiked up above ground level on garish gold metal poles. Here, the residents can escape outside and enjoy views out through the 100-year-old plane trees surrounding the scheme or back to their green, hairy building. The space offered in these outside rooms is a paradigm for escape; a retreat that is very different to the home, paradoxically so near and yet so far. Where apartments have their own balconies the railings are made of tightly packed vertical timber poles set into the concrete cantilever, lending a rustic sensibility to the overall massing. The joy of this housing scheme is its sense of adventure. Inside people may do what they wish with their homes, but from the outside this building, over time, will change and grow in a unique way, merging with nature, an emblem of its own green credentials. The next instalment from this architect will be the 'Flower Tower' in Paris, another 'green' building which will feature pre-planted balconies.

There was considerable resistance to the Montpellier scheme from the local authorities and the developer became nervous, concerned that no one would want to buy into the project, but all the units sold immediately. Perhaps this proves that people do not necessarily know that they want something adventurous and different until they are presented with a brave new idea.

High rise From New York to Sydney the skyscraper is here to stay. Nearly a century after the invention of the high-speed lift, these landmark buildings seem to define the whole spectrum of global cities. Our on-and-off love affair with the high rise remains ambivalent, though, particularly after the events of 11 September 2001 in New York. Clearly, while tall buildings allow for density of occupation, they can be subject to catastrophes, both manmade and natural. There are whole cities, such as Tokyo and San Francisco, that are built on geographic fault lines, meaning that at some point earth movement is inevitable. Fortunately modern engineering is becoming increasingly sophisticated and buildings can be designed to withstand extraordinary forces; this may not mean that the buildings remain undamaged, but it should ensure as far as possible the safety of the inhabitants. While land prices continue to soar and the incentive to live within an urban metropolis persists, the high rise will continue to be built.

There is an inherent glamour in living high above the streets, with a view looking out across a city. Seeing the ever-changing, 24-hour panorama of a cityscape becomes a cinematic experience. In the 1950s and 1960s, architects and planners talked of 'streets and gardens in the sky', but for many the reality of this translated into a grimy corridor and a windy balcony in a bleak and anti-social landscape. The obvious benefit of building tall is that more housing units can be fitted on to a given piece of land. As mentioned previously, however, Le Corbusier's ideal was that it would leave free the land at ground-level for parks or open spaces, but often this was not the reality – the surrounding land remained valuable and was used for further development. During the 1960s the industry geared itself towards constructing tall buildings quickly and cheaply. This was done by erecting frames of steel or concrete and then 'hanging' prefabricated façades from them. Poor fixing of the façades could result in major problems: at best, cold-bridging (where heat from the outside is conducted directly to the inside) and at worst, structural failure. It has taken decades to put the shortcomings of earlier high-rise developments behind us, but with more careful

planning and a better understanding of construction we are beginning to see a new era of high-rise housing for the twenty-first century.

Increasingly the challenge in the design of high-rise buildings is to marry sophisticated engineering practices with sculptural form. Towers will always be objects simply because of their scale in relation to their urban contexts and to the individual at street level. Their success has tended to be measured by the impact of their form and the amenities they offer. Unlike much mass housing, tower blocks tend to have controlled access points, via the lifts, and so offer an element of security. Parking may be situated in the basement along with shops, gyms and crèches. The scale of such an enterprise can often support a whole range of other activities at the lower levels.

Objects and icons
The Italian architect Renzo Piano, noted for his part in the design of the seminal Pompidou Centre in Paris in 1977, recently completed the Aurora Place office and housing tower in Sydney. It stands in the heart of the central business district next to other office buildings and close to the city's hotels. As one goes up the building, views open out to the harbour, the Botanical Gardens and beyond. At design stage, the architect noted that he was very aware that Jørn Utzon's Sydney Opera House – one of the city's symbols – was the nearest point of reference.

It is only a kilometre (under a mile) away and a dialogue between the two objects is inevitable. The tower is a striking slash on the horizon, clad in glass and terracotta tiles, which immediately differentiates it from its corporate neighbours. Indeed the sail-like form of the curved façade is a gesture that echoes the great curves of the Opera House. Each apartment has its own glazed balcony area that acts as a conservatory and buffer zone between inside and out. The design of the external glazed cladding system is quite complex, comprising glass louvre blinds that can be opened or shut for natural ventilation, according to the weather. The mechanisms were tested to withstand hurricane winds and torrential rain as they have to have a long lifespan. Piano's idea was to show that it is possible to have a tower block with sustainable mechanisms that are easily operated. Rooms do not have to be sealed and air-conditioned if they have been well designed.

These hi-tech principals were certainly not the generating force behind Australian Harry Seidler's 43-storey Horizon Apartments, also in Sydney. The tower appears as a series of white horizontal ribbons held in place by slender vertical columns. The 260 apartments were constructed from pressed concrete and the curved features are the apartment balconies. At the top the geometry twists in a wilful manner, suggesting that the building can be screwed

Left Harry Seidler's 'ribbon' architecture is seen again at his Hochhaus Neue Donau apartment building in Vienna, Austria. This concrete-framed tower contains 373 apartments over 34 floors and has fine vistas over the River Danube. *Opposite* Renzo Piano's Aurora Place tower is an elegant slice of a building in downtown Sydney. The lower housing block has a layer of glazed rooms on the façade which can be opened and closed to naturally modify the internal climate.

tight. The whole building has a nautical flavour and its graphic and glamorous quality, along with the awesome views over the harbour, appealed to the global market in which it was sold. There are different opinions as to whether a tower block can be truly site specific. It would be worrying to see such white towers exported to every place on the globe, but perhaps this one can be considered specific to Sydney, with its seemingly perfect weather and lifestyle.

In the city of Malmo, Sweden, Spanish architect and engineer Santiago Calatrava is building a new tower called 'Turning Torso'. The name and form of the building appear to have been derived from a sculpture made by Calatrava resembling a body. This has been translated into a twisting shape that holds nine cubic elements stacked one on top of the other and spiralling upwards. These contain around 400 living units that can be individually customized.

The plan for each floor resembles the end of a fountain pen, with a circular servicing core placed centrally. This necessitates radial partitions within the apartments that inevitably affect the plan options, some of which look quite uncomfortable. This particular tower has not been completed, but by its own admission the 'objectness' of the building, set on a flat quayside, is the main attraction. The views from the top will be amazing, but will people enjoy looking at it? According to its marketing hype, this building has come to represent a projection of the future, though it is doubtful if it can ever quite fulfil this promise.

The individuality of the tower block is less of a problem in cities where it is the predominant building type. In the newly developed mega-city of Shanghai hundreds of tower blocks, most of them unremarkable, are springing up everywhere, as they did in Hong Kong in the 1970s. Currently under construction is the Shanghai World Financial Centre by KPF Architects, a large multinational company based in New York and London. At a projected height of 460m (1,509ft), when completed in 2005 it could be the tallest building in the world. While most of the space will hold offices, there is talk of placing a hotel and penthouses at the top, offering some of the most spectacular panoramic views on the planet. The sleek, pencil-shaped tower is characterized by the 50m (164ft) diameter cylinder cut out of the top of the building. Already known as the 'moon gate', it is said that this form refers to an ancient Chinese lucky charm. But when an object is transposed from a human scale to a giant one, it ceases to be the same thing and verges on the banal.

Perhaps the idea of building tall remains more interesting than the results. Certainly we are used to a lot of generic office-type buildings, many of which are repetitive extrusions clustered together in development zones. The high-rise housing block has to work much harder if it wants to differentiate itself as a place of inhabitation rather than just a commercial expression.

Cities within cities The desire to create mega-housing schemes, or mini-cities, now appears to have been sated after much trial and error. Often attempts to fabricate new city centres or urban districts, these visions tended to suffer from the problem of uniformity. Back in the 1960s, a radical group of young architects calling themselves Archigram were dreaming of 'Walking Cities' and making psychedelic drawings of huge buildings which appeared to have legs. Places such as Chandigarh in India and Brasilia in Brazil had just been built and were singular visions of new cities. In London, the Barbican – a concrete homage to Le Corbusier comprising housing, a conference centre and an arts complex – was completed as late as the 1980s, though it had first been conceived of over 20 years earlier. It remains a seductive citadel, embedded in the City of London, though to this day the public complain of not being able to find their way around it. There now appears to be less investment in the ideals that inspired an earlier generation to build brave new worlds. In part this has to do with the

fact that there is less space on which to build; green space is sacred and legislation prevents development. Also the agents of development are less likely to be state bodies and so huge zonal construction projects are virtually impossible.

Yet there are instances of a masterplan or grand project serving to regenerate the cityscape, especially where there is a need for the denser inhabitation of a neighbourhood. In Vienna, four redundant but magnificent 100-year-old gasometers on the outskirts of the city have been transformed into a new neighbourhood comprising apartments, offices, a cultural centre, shops and a city archive. Austrian architect Coop Himmelbau and Jean Nouvel, who is based in Paris, both worked on turning the former derelict buildings into a new urban quarter. The circular structure of the gasometers has been retained and left open to form giant courtyards and the apartments face both inwards and outwards. Adjacent to the gasometers sits a curiously shaped, 22-storey glazed tower. Geometric dexterity is one of Himmelbau's trademarks and here he has created a dynamic tension between the almost Neo-Classical presence of the circular buildings and the twenty-first-century, shard-like tower, which has no decoration and reflects the environment in its mirrored cladding. The scheme forges complex cross-overs between its parts, thus avoiding becoming diagrammatic and programmed. The potential for new connections and conversions is embedded within the fabric as people can wander from one zone to another. The project is also commendable in so much as it represents a huge financial investment in a part of the city otherwise destined to decay. This draws in new residents and creates an infrastructure for jobs.

When designing a low-cost public housing development in Gifu, Japan, conceptual New York architects Diller and Scofidio decided not question the formality of the housing block in an obvious manner. A tight budget meant that the architects could not design a constructionally complex building, so they embarked upon a series of small-scale tactics which would affect the appearance of the whole. The structure is made of poured concrete and a total of 15 interlocking towers

contain a total of 104 units disposed at a slight angle
to each other. Each apartment has a façade made of
perforated metal panels and opening windows,
which overlap one another like giant wall-hung
cladding tiles. The height at which each panel is hung
drops from one unit to the next, a simple move that
creates a dynamic tension across the façade and
suggests movement, hence the name of the project:
Slither. This kind of architecture creates an
uncompromising and gritty environment. Yet the
very fact that it incorporates small changes and
details at the level of the individual dwelling, not
necessarily obvious from the exterior, means that
there is a sensitivity to human scale and inhabitation.
Much of the architects' other work has been
concerned with creating spaces that respond to
electronic communication. Here they concentrated
on the slippage between order and chaos; it is as
though the project is in a state of flux, captured just
as the formerly solid structure is beginning to melt.

For some reason the Dutch have long been
the harbingers of good housing design. Their
appreciation for well-conceived contemporary
housing has meant that demand for it is high: in the
city of Amsterdam alone over the past ten years
major house-building programmes have resulted in a
number of interesting projects of various scales,
many sited on reclaimed land. The Borneo-
Sporenburg scheme is particularly worth looking at
in detail. It was conceived of as a dockland
development containing 2,500 dwelling units, mostly
completed by 2000. The masterplan designated an
area of low-density housing, referred to as 'the
carpet', which is broken up by high-density housing
blocks that are dubbed 'meteorites'. One of these is
a vast building know to locals as 'the whale'.
Designed by de Architekten Cie, it sits surrounded
by water on two sides and has a twisting, folding
geometry. While it has none of the organic, sensuous
qualities of nature's largest mammal, it does have the
bulk and presence. It is not what you might call
beautiful, either. Yet the façade, which turns into the
roof, is tiled in zinc scales that glisten in the sun, and
the reflection from the water creates a sense of
movement. The building also appears to be held up
off the ground, as its underbelly is revealed sloping

down to a point of support. The windows are modular and shuffle in a syncopated rhythm across the façade in lines. The courtyard found at the heart of the project is a slightly unsettling space which feels very overlooked. If the building is not immediately appealing it does not necessarily matter. The apartments inside are well designed and affordable, and the fact that the building is so well known is a bonus. The scale and form of the building are overtly sculptural while the low-rise housing creates a textured landscape. Further along the harbour is another similar block, called Piraeus. Here the construction is brick and, while it also has a dynamic sculptural form, the overall language is heavier. It contains 300 dwellings created for a housing association. There are only two types of window in the whole project, ensuring huge economies of scale and consistent quality. The presence of water again enhances the sculptural effect of the building and suggests the seductive idea that it is floating.

Above The houses in the See Saw estate in Sussex, England, combine a traditional form with an eclectic use of materials, resulting in a collection of homes with a personality not obviously historicist.

Opposite The image of the cul-de-sac is a familiar sight the world over. From the air, individual homes surrounded by gardens creep across the landscape as far as the eye can see.

The rise of the box 'When you look at a ticky tacky box the first thing you see is a car; on the whole they are well designed, well made and modern. The kitchen will be full of the latest appliances and the lounge will contain the latest audiovisual equipment. People live in what they are offered. If they are not offered anything else what choice do they have?' Sir Terence Conran

Perhaps one of the most depressing responses to the question of mass housing has been the proliferation of the 'brick box'. These parodies of homes, clustered together to form estates, with often comically inappropriate pastoral names, litter the countryside in many countries. This global phenomenon is characterized by the desire to recreate a local historical vernacular. In the United Kingdom there is a horrid hybrid known as 'Tudorbethan'; in the United States it might be 'Ranch style' or 'New England style'; in Australia it is 'Colonial style'. The houses tend to huddle around curvy roads or cul-de-sacs, with individual garages and front gardens that are laid out to create the

impression of an idealized community. Often the houses are cheaply and badly made. Their architectural 'features' are merely tacked on to the surface and the very quality of timelessness and solidity they aspire to is entirely missing from the construction. These developments are to be criticized not for their attempt to make the world a better place, but for not believing that there are more appropriate solutions. It seems the house-buying public are not made aware of alternative ways of living; nor are they aware of some of the issues surrounding the environment and sustainability that must be addressed by the construction industry sooner or later.

Complex social and psychological elements determine our desire to own a home that is safe, comfortable and aspirational. Terence Conran's observation that within these historically themed worlds sits cutting-edge product design in the form of cars, stereos, computers and white goods, is very revealing. It can be seen as an indicator of the conflicting wish to live in the present day and in the past simultaneously – between an exciting but uncharted future and a collective nostalgia. This is fuelled by the kind of advertizing produced by developers, which lures and seduces people into buying their perfect lives. Many such developments are offered to the consumer as the ultimate in luxury, comfort and safety. Pick up any property newspaper and you will see promises not just of prime accommodation, but also of a whole lifestyle experience. A fine line exists between catering for our aspirations of an ideal life and cynically selling empty dreams. There appears to be a tacit acknowledgement by many developers that sustainability, contemporary aesthetics and innovation will not sell to a mass market. Why do people seem to resist homes that attempt to redefine twenty-first-century living?

Demographics and design As for all advertizing campaigns, homebuyers are segmented into different types and classes. The imagery used to sell urban apartments is aimed at well-paid professionals and often shows a highly sexualized environment filled with desirable objects and supermodels, suggesting that a seductive moment is just around the corner. On the other hand, the advertizing for family houses tends to concentrate on the traditional bricks and mortar, the amount of garden and open space and particularly on the kitchen and bathroom fittings – never mind that the insulation is poor and there are no shops nearby. The developers of retirement homes often try to create an image of tranquillity, conjured up by cosy familiar corners. Like all commercial enterprises the housing industry needs to use advertizing to reach its market, but it seems that the script has not changed for 20 years.

During the late 1980s and much of the 1990s the 'loft' phenomenon drove a new wave of urban interventions that regenerated old buildings. Developers or individuals would acquire a disused urban building, carve it up into empty shell spaces and renovate the infrastructure and common parts. Homebuyers could then purchase their space and fit it out exactly as they wished. This gave people the chance to be creative with their living environments and to

employ designers who were often young and inventive, and for whom this might well be their first commission. For a period, cities from New York to Manchester and Berlin to Barcelona benefited from this new wave of innovative appropriation. So successful was the idea that genuine opportunities afforded by this concept were often lost as prices went up. Developers found they could get higher returns if they actually fitted out the spaces themselves. Hence the term 'loft style' came into being, referring to a minimal pallete of materials that vaguely imitates the iconic qualities of the best conversions. Those who can afford to live in these newly discovered city-centre locations are often professionals. Those that have families or are on low incomes are forced to look outside the cities, often at new developments and small 'starter homes'. This is not to say that the conversion of disused buildings is over; indeed, numerous office buildings that are 20 or 30 years old no longer meet the requirements of hi-tech integrated operations, but can be easily transformed into apartments. It is a question of who gets there first.

New housing models The search for new models of housing and communities goes on. As a species, we seem to have an apparently endless task in redefining the way we choose to inhabit our world. Architecture and design have always contributed to the process of colonization, forming an integral part of a cultural framework. The search for better homes is a search for better lives. This does not always mean bigger or more expensive homes. What it does mean is some kind of shared ideology or, more simply, an idea that can be easily understood and experienced by those who become the inhabitants.

One recent and ongoing suburban development that attempts to create a new, design-conscious community is to be found in Prospect on the edge of Colorado in the United States (see p.138). Masterminded by designer Mark Sofield and developer Kiki Wallace, it stands out as a very different kind of vision for suburban living. Visitors remark that there is perhaps something a little disquieting about the sense of familiarity and quirky

perfection. This may spring from the pristine condition of the houses and gardens and the notable camaraderie of the inhabitants. However this is no Celebration, the Disney version of Prospect. Here there is a rejection of twee ordinariness and a healthy disrespect for the establishment. The styles of the houses built here are a mixture, ranging from pared-down historical to gymnastic deconstruction. It is no secret that this particular development is seen as an experiment; they talk about it as being the DNA for New Urbanism. The guidelines for inhabitants wishing to build their own houses constitute more of a manifesto than a shopping list of requirements, encouraging expression and individual taste over conformity. Each new home has a story attached which will depend on the client, the designer and the narrative they have made together. An example of this is one house that is fondly nicknamed 'The Bat Cave' by locals, referring to its black façade; other nicknames include 'The Death Star' and 'The Stealth House'. In addition to the spirit of bravado there is also space; the plots are

large and the houses generous. In the United States, people can afford to build big in the provinces where the cost of land is not prohibitive. So it seems that it is possible to create a fresh and invigorating living environment, which is sufficiently eclectic to allow traditional styles to mix with the cutting edge. The success of this particular development seems to be down to the partnership between developer and client as well as the attraction of creating something different. This experiment is not so much a blueprint for others in terms of style, so much as an appeal for understanding on behalf of local communities who desire original new housing.

Prefabrication A spate of new housing schemes built in England over the last few years shows that innovation and style is not just the remit of the wealthy. Today there is less and less government-built social housing and it has been replaced by housing co-operatives and associations. The Peabody Trust has a long history, dating back to Victorian times, of building economical, low-income

Above The sleek interior of this new apartment in London's Docklands epitomizes 'loft style' as interpreted by modern developers. Despite its generous living spaces, luxurious fittings and panoramic views over the city, it is somehow lacking in character.

INCORRIGIBLE CIR

housing, the majority of which still stands. One of its most recent projects was innovative both in terms of aesthetics and construction. Sited on the edge of London's central business district in a grey, semi-industrial zone, Murray Grove provides 74 flats for key workers, such as teachers and policemen, at affordable rents. Taking inspiration from the Japanese construction industry, architects Cartwright Pickard cut down the length of time taken to complete the programme on site by prefabricating modular units in a factory, then slotting them into place. Each housing unit was completely finished inside, right down to the wiring, and tested before being driven to the site. Once fixed in place on the simple concrete-pad foundation, the units were clad in terracotta tiles on the street side and timber boarding on the other. The footprint of the building is an L shape creating a garden in the centre. This is overlooked by the bedrooms which have floor-to-ceiling sliding windows and balconies. Due to minute attention to detail, the proposal goes a long way to dispelling the myth that all prefabricated interiors feel like caravans.

The access to each flat is via an external covered walkway, which is reached via a lift on the corner of the site. The circular steel-and-glass structure is floodlit at night, emphasizing the kit-of-parts concept of the design. Possibly the exterior suffers from an industrial uniformity and displays some of the wear and tear, even vandalism, usual on inner city sites. Yet the robustness of the whole is a pleasing and clever reinterpretation of a genre, providing excellent accommodation in the centre of a densely populated city.

A similar proposition found in Birmingham is known as Caspar – City-centre Apartments for Single People at Affordable Rents (see p.141). This building was also built by a charitable trust, the Joseph Rowntree Foundation and it too has experimented with prefabrication, in this case the bathroom pods. The building takes the form of a big shed: there are two parallel accommodation blocks with a covered courtyard atrium in the centre animated by bridge elements and balcony access. The whole of this semi-indoor courtyard is timber-clad, lending a Scandinavian sensibility to the volume. It

also functions as a community space; people can look out and see others coming in and out of their apartments. Externally the building is made of brick punctured by a regular matrix of steel windows. The pitched roof, with its open sides, is a quirky element that nods towards a more traditional vernacular but distinguishes itself from its neighbours. This image of the contemporary warehouse is a popular one and when seen from the nearby canal makes perfect sense. London-based architects AHMM note that the overall diagram of the scheme is seen as a possible blueprint for future projects, thus reinforcing the power of architecture and design to shape the cities we live in.

Mass housing and sustainability

The word sustainability has become a fashionable buzzword, though for many its meaning remains elusive. In terms of building it could be said that the emphasis is to seek the maximum architectural value with the minimum environmental impact. The RIAS's (Royal Incorporation of Architects in Scotland) environmental policy states that it 'Promotes a lifecycle approach to the design and construction of buildings and their components, which does not endanger environmental or personal health, and which respects biodiversity, intergenerational responsibility and social equity.' The question seems to be a balancing act between the need to create more infrastructure while at the same time preserving and conserving natural resources.

It is easy to see how waste accumulates on a daily basis within the home, and there are now easier ways in which to separate domestic waste so that it can be recycled. But who considers what happens to buildings and homes when they are demolished? In the past nearly all building-clearance waste was put into skips and dumped. Today much more thought goes into those components that can be taken away and reused in some form.

Another consideration when creating a sustainable home is running costs, which reflect the efficiency of the home in conserving energy. Lighting, cooking and heating all give out heat, much of which is wasted. Water is also often wasted. The design of systems to conserve water and power is critical to

the success of a sustainable building. Some ideas are very simple, such as switches and sensors that turn off heating and lighting if a space is not occupied. In places like Arizona where it gets very hot, there are systems that recycle water and use it to feed the garden. At the fundamental level, however, one might ask if it is appropriate to want traditional gardens in the desert. Perhaps this is the nub of the problem. Traditional patterns of domestic building do not always translate easily into a 'green' building. People have to want something different.

Architects Baumschlager and Eberle have designed a rigorous housing scheme in the city of Innsbruck, Austria, as part of their research into low-cost sustainable housing. They claim that we now have the technology to realize comfortable living environments while reducing the consumption of natural resources. The housing blocks are situated on the outskirts of the city close to precious woodlands. Six blocks in total were built, all with courtyards at their centres. The apartments are characterized by their external balconies and shutters which open and close to afford protection from either sun or wind. The shutters are individually controlled, energy-saving devices. The saw-tooth roofs are also solar collectors, which heat huge tanks of water in the basement which are then used to meet domestic requirements. Maximum energy efficiency is achieved inside each apartment with triple glazing, ventilation units and heat-exchanger pumps. One of the potential problems to be overcome was educating the occupants in the use of their new homes. A few people found the shutters too oppressive and removed them. Most, though, were happy with their apartments and appreciative of the lower running costs, proving that it is possible to live comfortably in an energy-saving environment and giving weight to the argument that sustainable development is a feasible way forward.

There is perhaps another agenda behind these buildings: an obsession with order and control. Each building is the same, and when closed up they appear to be abstract grey slabs stacked on top of each other. Once inhabited, however, the shutters are an index to the way people are living inside.

High density eco-housing On a very different scale, the Greenwich Millennium Village in London (see p.142) attempts to create a high-density model for housing that is popular and 'green'. Architects Procter Matthews designed 189 residential units employing a modular solution. Here the use of materials was key to creating a new aesthetic. Many of the houses are laid out in terraces and have striking corrugated aluminium roofs and colourful façades. The use of louvres, solar shades and cedar panelling enriches the façades while avoiding any reference to the past. The coloured panels are made of recyclable, honeycombed aluminium which has been rendered and the cedar cladding comes from managed sources. The buildings were all prefabricated and brought to site before being assembled as a kit of parts.

In plan the houses are compact but they have a generous ambience owing to their high ceilings and full-height doors and windows. The ground floor contains a cloakroom and storage space as well as the L-shaped kitchen and living area, opening on to a private courtyard. A staircase leads up to two bedrooms and a shared bathroom and there is a further room in the roof. Some of the units are live/work spaces that back on to the car park, the roof of which is used as a garden. The car park itself was designed as a buffer zone between the houses and busy surrounding roads. It also means that people have to walk to their homes from the car, freeing up the streets for pedestrian access. The homes have been designed to use only 50 per cent of the energy that a standard British home requires. To some the results are a little too child-like; the

Above left The timber-clad atrium of the Caspar housing project in Birmingham by AHMM contains a series of access decks and bridges. From the outside, the building has a shed-like appearance.
Above right A system of balconies and shutters defines the façades of these seven-storey apartment blocks by Baumschlager and Eberle on the outskirts of Innsbruck, Austria.

primary colour scheme is anything but subtle. Yet this housing is innovative, cheaper to build and more energy efficient than most and has been embraced by the community that lives there.

Another completed phase in the development demonstrates a different attitude to the same requirements. Swedish architect Ralph Erskine, who designed the masterplan of the area, showed how a new development could have a dense structure of streets, alleys and courtyards similar to a historical European model. His apartments are grouped in tall buildings that create a strong physical edge to the whole project. The housing blocks are characterized by their irregular massing and barrel-vaulted roofs; the tallest are 11 storeys high. A seemingly random pattern of balconies implies that the buildings developed over time. This fits into Erskine's idea of creating places that are human and local rather than abstract and empty. From the outside, each apartment can be understood as an individual element within the matrix, rather than a coordinate on a grid; within, the spaces are urbane and elegant. Like the other projects in the development there was much emphasis on prefabrication and energy-saving design. Household water is recycled and purified and used for flushing toilets, while rainwater is collected to feed planting. All commodities are metred and the data collected to review the

performance of the houses. The landscaping here is also important. There is an ecological park featuring a large lake complete with its own island bird sanctuary. In itself this use of a 'brownfield site' represents a bold step forward in the regeneration of urban wastelands.

At Bill Dunster's fashionably named 'Bed Zed' project in south London, energy efficient homes have been designed so that an even temperature can be maintained inside. This is achieved through massively insulated walls and triple-glazed windows. The architecture of Bed Zed is one that combines a sense of playfulness as well as providing a working model for future developments of mass eco-housing. Viewed from the air the development may look a little repetitive, but the interior spaces of the homes are light and generous, allowing inhabitants the freedom to customize them however they choose.

Humanist concerns This serves to remind us that architecture exists only as a backdrop to human affairs, which are imbued with multifarious desires and demands. Architecture can bridge the metaphorical world of ideas with the concrete world of physical expression, but this does not always lead to a true or happy environment. The architecture itself is dumb. It requires inhabitation and interpretation to activate it and make it live.

Above **The primary colours and robust forms of Procter Matthews' eco-houses at the Greenwich Millenium Village result in an almost Lego-like aesthetic.** *Above right* **Strong forms and colours define another housing development at Greenwich by Ralph Erskine.** *Below right* **In south London Bill Dunster Architects have created an ecologically sustainable suburb known as Bed Zed – the Beddington Zero Energy Project.**

6. Case Studies

Elektra House and Studio

London, United Kingdom, Adjaye/Associates

When plans for it were first published, this modest house caused something of a furore in the design press: it was praised by some for its individualism and criticized by others for its uncompromising philosophy. The clients ended the debate by saying that they were very happy in the house and could not understand the strength of feeling that was being expressed. Such is the power of an iconic architectural statement.

The house was designed by Adjaye/Associates for an artist and a sculptor who wanted a family home on a budget. The site is an urban infill, set into the gritty landscape of East London. From the outside the façade is a black panelled wall set off the pavement on a concrete plinth. There are no windows. This in itself suggests a more industrial programme than a conventional house; there is no obvious reference to the idea of 'home'. The monolithic construction is clad in special dark-coloured resin-coated plywood which has the appearance of steel plates. The front door is reached by passing through a gate to the side of the building and walking down a narrow passage to a small courtyard.

Once you are inside a completely different experience awaits. The interior is bright and airy, reminiscent of a loft space inserted into another building. There is no real sense of location, not least because you cannot see out so there is no point of reference. The ground floor has been arranged to maximize the open-plan living zone. The service areas are positioned in smaller, subservient spaces. The kitchen is treated as though it were an extension, neatly occupying a small, single-height box. The only natural light here is brought in through a rooflight in the ceiling. Next to this is a built-in dining niche which has a view into the timber-decked lightwell along the back of the site. Overall the architect has manipulated the way light is brought into the home very carefully – light is either reflected into the rooms or filtered from above. The glass roof above the dining space creates an abstract connection with nature – when it rains you can see it splashing on the glass – without actually becoming a conservatory. Behind the main façade is a double-height slot which is also roof-lit, bringing daylight into the family room.

The materials used within the home reflect the budget; concrete, painted white walls and knotty pine timber. This fascination with 'everyday' materials leads to a kind of austerity that some would find alienating. Here, however, it forms a space which the inhabitants can dress according to their own taste and inclination. In that sense it is a raw space which carries the same connotations as art galleries created from old warehouses, perhaps a reflection of the clients' own interests.

The upstairs is reached by a long pocket stair which is placed behind a flank wall. There are three compact rooms and a bathroom. Here the floor is finished in pale timber, the only natural material in the building. The doors are all full height, providing a generous sense of scale. Once again there are only two windows giving on to the side alley, though each space has its own skylight. Built-in closets usefully conceal the clutter of everyday life, leaving a series of simple cellular spaces.

This is an extreme response to the question of making domestic space, and it could never be described as homely. Yet it remains a triumph of individualism and resourceful thinking. To build an 'ideas house' for a limited budget in one of the world's most expensive capital cities is no mean feat. It also illustrates the importance of patronage; that clients entrust the architect with the business of testing concepts and developing a new language for the places in which we live.

Opposite **With its austere façade, the Elektra House is an enigmatic presence on the street. It appears as a very distinct object set within a context of traditional brick homes and remains a controversial experiment.**

Above left A view through open doors into two bedrooms reveals the simple ordering of spaces. *Above right* A double-height slot brings light into the living space from above and separates the bedrooms from the main façade. *Opposite* The glazed wall on the garden side appears as a lightbox to the outside world by night and by day collects light for the dining area below.

Sheep Farm House

Victoria, Australia, Denton Corker Marshall

This extraordinary house of concrete and glass is set within the bush terrain of southern Australia. How can one make a landmark on such an open and empty site? The structure, over 217m (712ft) long, acts as a wind break and contains the home at its core: the architecture responds to the vast scale of its surroundings while providing a place of shelter. Seen from the southwest the language of folded concrete creates an industrial landscape. On the other side the building is glazed, affording panoramic views from the inside. Along this aspect the roof is cantilevered and supported by a row of raked steel columns. The roof appears as something much less solid, like a canvas tent stretched across a row of poles.

The choice of industrial materials at first seems at odds with the idea of integrating with the surroundings, but this harsh terrain demands a robust response. The first-time visitor could well be confused as to whether it is a house at all. After all, a couple of stainless-steel storage tanks stand along the flank wall and the

front entrance is a skewed opening in the concrete façade with a bright yellow door floating behind. There is no front doorstep or path indicating that it is a way in. Yet it is precisely this enigmatic sense that gives the house its commanding presence. By night the house acts as a beacon in the wilderness; the pitched roof floats above the building, which politely shelters beneath. This project is more than simply a house – it is a place on the map and signifies a destination.

Above The abstract geometric form of Sheep Farm House reads as an elemental concrete fold in the landscape. *Opposite above* The front door is hidden inside the monolithic concrete wall. The main kitchen/living area is an open-plan loft-like space. *Opposite below* Along the northeast aspect, the roof is supported by a row of skinny steel beams.

The interior layout of the house is far more straightforward than the exterior suggests. A series of bedrooms, bathrooms and service spaces sits behind the monolithic angled wall, opening up into a loft-like living space flowing into the kitchen area. The simplicity of the external materials is continued inside the home, which has terrazzo floors and dark panelled walls. The house is functional but full of character. The design creates a number of different experiences by manipulating the way daylight is brought inside. A slot between the angled exterior and the box containing the cellular rooms is top-lit so that dramatic shafts of light animate the corridor. By contrast, the open living area, which is shaded from direct sun by the overhang, gives on to a panorama; the light here is more diffused.

On a practical level the house is suited to a variety of different living patterns. The bedrooms are placed at either end of the plan, which is ideal for guests who do not wish to intrude. An office is positioned on the left of the front door, allowing business to be conducted from home but in such a way as not to interfere with the everyday running of the house. Perhaps the most homely touch is the fireplace, which acts as a low dividing wall within the main living space. When it is not operational the wall is static, reading as a screen. When the weather turns, the fire is lit and the furniture is drawn up towards the flickering flame. This gathering around the fire evokes the long history of the hearth as a focal point for family life although here, admittedly, it has been abstracted and offset by the self-conscious nature of the design.

Overall Sheep Farm House is an excellent example of a home that synthesizes a strong philosophical idea – about living in the Outback – with an elegant and generous living arrangement. It demonstrates that a modern approach can provide both an ordered environment that maximizes the pleasure of the rural setting and an intimate, sometimes snug, interior world.

Above left A corridor is formed between the angled external concrete wall and the accommodation block within. Light is filtered from above. *Above right* The northeastern terrace is shaded by the solid cantilevered roof; the run of angled struts poking through the edge makes a rhythmic gesture. *Opposite* Marking the boundary, a concrete flank wall extends away from the house, opening up to frame the hillside beyond. Three industrial stainless steel storage vessels form a seductive sculptural composition to the right-hand side.

Above *Approached from raised ground the house appears to be set into the landscape.* Left *The courtyard entrance to the house is sparse and formal. Over time, however, the grove of trees will provide an elegant shady counterpoint to the architecture.* Right *The kitchen reads as a piece of cabinetry set into the back wall. A floating island containing the sink is multifunctional and can be used as a breakfast bar. The long wall to the outside is a series of solid panels holding storage and floor-to-ceiling glass windows.* Far right *The form of the house is revealed from this side. Behind the angled concrete façade the sleeping and bathing quarters are expressed as dark boxes, while the living space appears transparent, as though just using the roof for shelter.*

The Red House
London, United Kingdom, Tony Fretton Architects

Set back from the River Thames in Chelsea, London, this unique new house occupies a site that was once occupied by two 1950s houses; these were demolished to create a clean slate.

From the street the house is curious and formal. It is joined to the neighbouring building on one side and has an almost blank flank wall on the other. The geometric, box-like façade is clad in red French limestone that lends the house a distinct gravitas. There is a strong symmetrical arrangement of forms and windows, beginning at the base, which is topped by a grand central window at first-floor level, and continuing to the parapet line, which completes the façade. Three smaller windows punched into the central block disrupt the exact symmetry. Above, a series of lightweight boxes are set back from the roof line giving a clue to another world beyond. This kind of architecture is a fusion between a Classical sensibility and an artful reinterpretation of tradition. Some might say that the façade is rather cold and forbidding, while others might enjoy its robust presence; either way, it avoids being a pastiche of its nineteenth-century neighbours. One of the overriding themes of the building is the craftsmanship that has been lavished on each detail. From the careful jointing of the stone on the outside to the beautifully made window casements on the inside, there is a consistency of thought and finish.

The house is entered through a tiny courtyard that opens up into a formal stairwell with an oval patterned stone floor. This leads into the ground-floor living area which includes a large, partly open-plan kitchen. A garage and a mini-flat are also contained at this level, which drops down to the basement. The scale of the circulation and public spaces is extremely generous and almost decadent. The grand entertaining room on the first floor is reached via the staircase, and recalls the idea of a *piano nobile*, a raised main floor found in many Italian palazzos. This important space has windows at the front as well as at the back and to one side, with a fireplace set into the remaining internal wall. The ceiling here is a sensuous curved surface specially commissioned from artist Mark Pimlott. In fact, the collaboration between architect and artist has resulted in a number of installations around the building, including a canvas on the soffit of the dining-room and a clear Perspex washstand in the bathroom. The most surprising feature of all is the cocktail bar in the main entertaining room, secretly tucked in behind the fireplace wall and lined with glass shelves filled with bottles which glow under the discreet fibre-optic lighting.

On reaching the top floor of the house the formality gives way to a more relaxed arrangement of rooms around a courtyard. The master bedroom has its own walk-in wardrobe and a large bathroom with a roof terrace on both sides. The garden consists of an enclosed roof terrace with a hot-tub overlooking London and a small tropical hot-house which is passed on the way up the stairs. Two guest bedrooms and a bathroom are neatly housed to one side of the floor, hugging the next-door building. The design of these spaces makes the most of the light and air by having floor-to-ceiling glass windows that capture breathtaking views but are not overlooked. The detailing of these lightweight roof structures is crisp and contemporary, striking a different note within the overall composition of the house.

The ambitious aims of this project have been exquisitely executed. An idea about materials, spatial organization and detailing appears to have informed every decision the designer and client have made together. The result is a masterpiece, representing more than just bricks and mortar; the onlooker may draw inspiration from the balance between rigour and playfulness, between traditional references and modern shapes.

Opposite From the street, the massing of the Red House respects the lines of its historic neighbours, though the form and details are clearly contemporary. It is an enigmatic building, with one foot in the past, not wanting to make too much of a statement.

Previous page An external steel and glass deck leads down to the back garden via an elegant curved stair. Opposite The precise detailing of the junctions where the floor meets a wall or window are particularly important to the success of the project. Above The bedrooms and bathrooms on the top floor are airy, light-filled spaces. Above left The gridded canvas ceiling of the dining room was made by artist Mark Pimlot who collaborated with the architect on many aspects of the house. Below left The lightweight rooftop accommodation is visible above the trees.

Danielson House

Nova Scotia, Canada, Brian MacKay-Lyons

This elegantly crafted house has a remote setting on the side of a cliff on Cape Breton, Nova Scotia – not a particularly easy location to reach. The house was designed by Brian MacKay-Lyons for a couple who for four years had camped out in a rustic shed that stood on the site. The design is a canny experiment in creating a generous and delightful living environment on a tight budget. Inside, the building can be opened up or closed off depending on the time of year, and this flexibility alludes to a way of life that responds to the seasons.

From a distance the house has a kind of familiarity, somewhere between a flat-pack shed and a modern cottage. It is very much a kit of parts, using existing off-the-shelf components assembled in a surprising and innovative way. The idea was to create a lofty volume that was enclosed and protected by a large corrugated steel roof that reads as a folded element wrapping over the cottage beneath. It suggests that the building underneath is living, and is being protected by the robust metal covering. There is nothing minimal or precious about this approach, and yet the result is by no means unsophisticated. The knowing collection of architectural elements, assembled in a particular way, reflects a beachcomber mentality. The slightly suburban window panels that provide an ocean view from within are interrupted by a timber-clad bay which has a chimney poking out of the top, a deliberate interruption of the façade by the internal function. The patchwork of infill panels reinforces the narrative that the house is a collection of parts.

The main building sits on a timber deck providing outside seating, and is counterbalanced to one side by a much smaller pavilion, which is called the belvedere. This miniature version of the house is used as a day-room or guest wing, a satellite to the mothership. In the summer the owners have been known to sleep outside beneath the stars, waking to the distant view of Newfoundland. The poetic tension between the larger building and its offspring suggests an organic relationship between the two, and helps anchor the buildings to the site. There is also a reference to

local timber boats, where the larger vessel is led out to sea by a smaller tug boat. All of these associations add to the experience of the place as an authentic home, perfectly set into its surroundings.

The clunkiness of the house from the outside gives little away about the generous living space within. One of the starting-points for designing the house was to ensure that running costs were kept to a minimum. As a result the the internal arrangement has been planned so that the bathroom, bedrooms and kitchen – the only spaces to have plumbing and central heating – are clustered together. (And because the expensive services were only in one corner of the building construction costs were also kept low.) This linear slot of accommodation can be shut off from the main barn-like space using a sliding door which, when closed, melds into the vertical timber-clad walls, creating a single pure volume. The bedrooms are nothing more than a bed and a wall of built-in storage, planned like a ship's cabin. These rooms make up only a third of the area of the house. By contrast the main space is divided into four structural bays which are open to the roof, where timber trusses and rafters have been left exposed, recalling a more traditional vernacular architecture. An intimate timber-lined nook has been created on the outside wall of the building; it contains a fireplace, a window and a bench to sit at and can be enclosed by sliding folding doors to create a minute snug in winter. The rest of the façade is glazed, maximising views across the ocean.

Opposite The Danielson House perches above the rocky shoreline of Cape Breton, Nova Scotia, where the forest meets the sea. From this distance it is unclear whether this is a new house or an extension to an existing building.

Above **External louvres can be manually operated from the outside of the house to provide solar shading within.** *Opposite above, left to right* **The formal composition of the house is balanced by the smaller satellite day-room which appears to have drifted away from the main building. A corrugated metal roof wraps around the building to form a protecting enclosure; the fireplace nook is clearly expressed on the outside as a timber-clad box. The main living space is uncluttered and open to the rafters above; the timber fireplace niche can be opened up or closed off to make a snug.** *Opposite below, left to right* **The fireplace is offset by a window and reading bench. A long sliding wall divides off the service zones of the house. When it is open, light floods in from the rear windows behind the kitchen.**

14–19 Rue des Suisses

Paris, France, Herzog and de Meuron

Swiss architects Jacques Herzog and Pierre de Meuron are well known for their elegant and sparse use of materials, combining utility with proportion and a refined aesthetic. Their social housing scheme in rue des Suisses in Paris is no different. The location is a slot within the smart but nondescript residential area of the fourteenth *arrondissement*. The footprint of the site is an elongated T shape. A seven-storey building is set into the street façade at the front, while a lower three-storey linear block makes a courtyard behind. A third wedge is squeezed into a corner and has its own presence on a side street, rue Jonquoy. All three structures are made from a basic concrete frame with separate balcony elements attached. There is also a flat designated for the concierge who monitors the building and arranges for ongoing maintenance.

From the front the building appears as a curious, sculptural, grey metallic object which has been gently folded along two vertical lines. Horizontal bands articulate the different floor levels, which are infilled with full-height perforated metal shutters. These can be opened and closed by the residents, graphically communicating who is in or out and allowing residents to be seen or to hide away. As a device it is a 'one-liner', yet it is visually so different to its polite neighbours that the effect is startling and intriguing. In the open position the folded shutters actually stick out over the line of the street, making new stripes and shadows on the façade. The main entrance itself is very discreet, just a single door finished in the same grey metal. The passage within is clad in bright-green reflective glass creating a surreal transition from the public realm into a semi-private one.

Away from the street and within the courtyard the theme of shuttered façades continues. Here they are sensuous, curved, slatted rolls, reminiscent of the tambours in an antique writing desk. The three-storey façade is modulated in timber waves held in place by sinuous metal sections. Behind these are deep, south-facing balconies with their own vertical railings which provide generous outdoor rooms accessed by full-height sliding doors. Both the deck

and the soffit above are clad in timber, adding a layer of nautical imagery to the experience. There are three ramped concrete entrances to the generous day-lit stairwells leading to the individual flats. The ground-floor apartments have additional accommodation to the rear, created by wedges around small yards within the buffer zone between the next-door building.

As a counterpoint to the long, low block and opposite its entrances, sit two maisonettes. They are designed as diagrammatic houses, a motif developed from the architects' earlier Rudin House (see p. 47): a pitched roof sits on a solid square block, and floor-to-ceiling windows on the ground floor are protected by full-height roll-down shutters. They sit discreetly within a gravelled courtyard that is simply landscaped with a handful of trees and a monolithic stone bench. In a way they are not necessary to the scheme, and yet their simple identity is a reminder that this is a project for people who live in homes and not just an anonymous address. The exposed concrete walls have been softened by climbing plants which grow up metal trelliswork.

The success of this 60-apartment development is the diversity of the accommodation it offers. The two tall blocks comprise sophisticated but compact urban studios, while the low building is better suited to families as its homes contain two bedrooms and the long balcony space. The architectural moves on the outside create modern and spacious interiors, enriched by the huge windows and the play of sunlight though the shutters. The detailing is simple to the point of minimal – there are no skirtings and door frames as such – and the accommodation provides an excellent blank canvas on to which people can paint their lives.

Opposite The façade of Herzog and de Meuron's apartment block at 14–19 rue des Suisses curves sinuously between its more traditional neighbours. The full-height perforated shutters create an ever-changing pattern depending on the preferences of the occupants.

Above Balconies at the rear are characterized by their special roll-top timber blinds which run in a grooved track. *Above right* Metal and timber shutters juxtaposed in the courtyard. *Centre right* From the rear courtyard the three elements of the project can be seen: the steel-clad structure facing rue des Suisses; the long, three-storey, balconied block; and the small maisonettes at street level. *Below right* The ground-floor apartments have small wedges of garden butting up to the boundary wall. *Opposite* Light filters through the chainmail mesh of the folding shutters.

Valley Center House

California, United States, Daly Genik Architects

The Valley Center House has been hailed as a 'phoenix' rising out of the ashes of a catastrophic wildfire. Perched 549m (1800ft) above sea-level, this new industrial-looking house has generous views over a citrus and avocado farm. Designers Daly Genik Architects have developed a strong typology for this home which owes as much to its spectacular location as to the aesthetics of the machine. It has been designed as an energy-conscious and deliberately challenging retreat. The house is laid out as three wings around a courtyard which contains a swimming pool. Two of the poolside arms are guest accommodation while the third contains the main living space and kitchen. Viewed from the open side of the courtyard, it could be mistaken for a motel complex, as each room is articulated as a box and these are staggered in plan, denoting separate identities within. Depending on the time of year, or even the time of day, the building can be permeable or sealed; mechanized folding wings open and close to allow light and heat into the building.

The construction sits on top of a continuous cantilevered concrete slab which raises it sufficiently off the ground that the inhabitants are able to survey the scenery below. More importantly, the building's construction is more or less fireproof, ensuring that its future is secure. The guest wings are clad in a corrugated grey concrete board which emphasizes the 'factory' language of the architecture. Large sliding aluminium panels can be moved across the windows, opening up the bedrooms to the courtyard and allowing air to circulate freely. The main spaces are protected using bi-folding perforated metal doors and cantilevered screens which act as sun shades.

From a distance, the entrance can be made out as a cut-out corner, with the body of the main living space projecting above, its wings outstretched. The landscaping around is rough and ready, almost 'as found', with no unnecessary manicuring. Tall slot windows, lined in yellow, pop up slightly above the line of the corrugated façade, implying that they too have been spliced in. In placing the pool in the centre of the three-sided courtyard the architects draw on a timeless tradition which uses the tranquil, calming effect of water to create meditative surroundings. As night falls the building is seductively reflected in the water, as though a mirror has been held up to it and there are two houses.

Inside, the living space is organized around a central square concrete column which houses the fireplace. The ceiling is left open, revealing the timber rafters and lending a more rustic sensibility to the room. At one end the open kitchen is simply planned, held within a timber niche. In front sits a modest dining table, on the axis with the back of the concrete flue. Around the fireplace a collection of leather chairs and a sofa are placed on top of a crafted rug. This juxtaposition of old and new suggests that this is more of a home than 'a machine for living in'. Yet from the outside, set within the rugged terrain, the building floats as though unsure about whether to land in this desolate spot.

This building illustrates the way in which technical innovation can sit comfortably with the notion of domestic space, inhabited by real people and eclectic furniture. The building itself is adaptable and responsive to the environment, but it is those who live there who control it. There is no predetermined comfort zone; it is up to the individual if he or she wishes to close a window or slide a door across, and the use of protective screens means that the luxury of fully glazed façades can be enjoyed when appropriate.

Opposite *The living room of the Valley Center House looks out on to an open courtyard containing the pool. The two guest wings, with their opening doors, fan out on either side. The landscaping of the internal courtyard subverts the symmetry of the composition by offsetting the pool to one side, allowing the steps alone to make an axial statement.*

Above left The windows pop up above the roof line and return back to form a skylight of sorts. *Above right* The entrance to the house has been cut into a corner, thus creating a covered porch. *Left* Shadows are cast on to the window wall of a guest bedroom, animating the more public space of the poolside with a cinematic gesture. *Opposite* By night the transparency of the metal grilles allows views right inside the living room. The large perforated aluminium shading panels are seen in their horizontal and open position, creating a mirror image in the reflecting pool of the courtyard.

Above Formed in a U shape, the kitchen has been kept simple. Most of the
storage is contained below the worktop with only a single metal shelf for pots
and pans. The timber roof structure adds to the rustic effect of the interior.
Opposite A concrete pillar, containing storage and a fireplace, divides the dining
area from the living room. The roughness of the materials makes reference to
the harsh landscape outside, while the clean lines of the furniture suggest
sophisticated elegance.

Aura House

Tokyo, Japan, FOBA

Aura House is an eccentric slot house wedged between two existing buildings in the heart of Tokyo. At night the translucent roof glows, drawing attention to itself, presenting itself as a curious object that appears to have landed from another planet and suggesting a very different programme from that of its conservative neighbours. The word 'aura' means the extension of one's being beyond the natural body, thus implying that the influence of the house reaches beyond its physical envelope.

The overall site plan is a mere 3.5m (11½ ft) wide by 21.5m (70ft) long and the structure comprises two massive sheer concrete walls that act as book ends. They are curved in shape and asymmetrical, each wall rising up to a high point at either end, and set diagonally opposite one another. A membrane roof has been stretched between the two walls creating a twisted, elastic form. The fabric roof allows the internal space to be flooded by light during the day, while at night the electric light within emanates outwards. Along one side the concrete wall is punctured by a large, circular window which acts as a porthole framing a single view out.

Within, the house is equally unusual. The concrete flank walls have been left exposed and are beautifully made. The bolt holes that held the original shuttering are still visible, a product of the construction process. The result is a series of panels, where the joint reads as a seam, with eight equally spaced circular indentations. The electrical sockets have been cast into the thickness of the concrete and have an elegant circular metal plate around the hardwiring. Perhaps the most surprising features are a series of tubes which span the two solid walls to create a quasi-ceiling plane on the second floor. They have been used to contain the air-handling system and the uplights which illuminate the roof.

The programme for the building is deliberately ambiguous. All three floors are open, with the staircase along one side of the room in the middle of the plan. FOBA claim that the house is deliberately devoid of kitchen, bathrooms and designated room functions. In a city such as Tokyo there are literally hundreds of restaurants and noodle bars in the neighbourhood, a bathhouse around every corner, even the notorious 'love' hotels nearby. The house then becomes a container for events and a few personal objects. The idea of a home has been reduced to its most basic level. The concept may seem hard to grasp, yet in such a densely populated city the idea of personal space is held at a premium, and it is this commodity that the project has maximized and celebrated to the full. It also means that the three floors can be taken over to create a working environment, a gallery or shop.

Perhaps the most seductive aspect of the house is revealed in the night-time photographs, in which cinematic shadows of the inhabitants are cast on to the glass façade, playing out the unscripted drama of domestic life.

Left *Cylindrical concrete beams set at different angles make the top floor of the house into a very particular place. The stretched fabric above creates the waterproof seal to the enclosure. Opposite Seen from the street at night the façade glows and the blurry figures of people can be seen inside.*

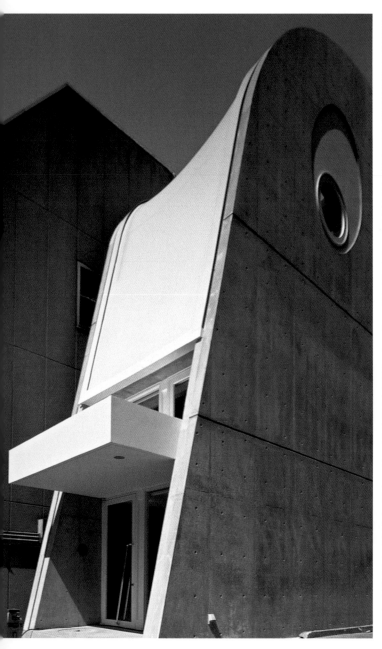

Above left Sheer concrete walls form the two sides of the building. A circular cut-out contains an offset porthole window at second-floor level. *Above right* The stretched membrane roof is pulled down to just above the front door. A white cantilevered slab forms a porch with the glazed door and wall set back beneath it.

Above From above, the light from the roof of Aura House draws attention to
the tiny slot which benignly twinkles amongst the irregular patchwork of
geometric windows that make up the rest of the city.

Plots 12 and 18, Borneo-Sporenburg

Amsterdam, The Netherlands, MVRDV

Over the past 20 years The Netherlands have embarked upon a number of large-scale urban building programmes, the most ambitious of which is called Borneo-Sporenburg, built on reclaimed land in Amsterdam's old harbour. The master plan, conceived by a landscape architectural practice, West 8, aimed to create a dense neighbourhood on two spits of land laced with narrow canals and dictated that terraces of houses would be constructed, all with the same footprint and a maximum height of 9m (30ft). A number of architects were approached to design the individual units which are grouped together in different arrangements to create a streetscape that is both controlled and varied.

Rotterdam-based practice MVRDV designed two of the houses, enigmatically referred to as plots 12 and 18. Both suggest ways in which slots of space can be divided in plan and section to create a variety of living and working zones. They also explore ideas of transparency, connecting the front of the house to the back. The house on plot 12 has been designed for a couple who may work from home. The plot measures 5m (16ft) wide by 16m (52ft) deep and at ground-floor level has been divided in two: the ramped 'alleyway' allows a visual link between the street and canal and serves as an occasional parking bay. By dividing the site in this way the architects have created two parallel zones, one with slabs of horizontal space that occupy four floors and the other, above the 'alleyway', occupied by boxes for contained activities. The entrance is taken up by a dog-leg stair that services all floors. At the lower level is a kitchen/dining-room that overlooks the canal and opens up into a linear, protected yard. At ground-level a work space connects to the street. On the first floor a bedroom pod overhangs the parking slot and another long room, of flexible function, opens into a double-height space. The top floor houses a bathroom and

Right Looking down the canal, the façades of the new houses at Borneo-Sporenburg are repeated in different sequences creating a laminated effect.

main living room and has doors on to a balcony, on the roof of one of the 'boxes'. This complex grid of interlocking cubes creates a far more dynamic living arrangement than is normally found in a terraced house.

In a similar vein the house on plot 18, which measures 4.2m (14ft) wide by 16m (52ft) deep, has been conceived as a series of floating cubes held between the two flank walls. The plan of the house is arranged about a central staircase dividing the house in two, front and back, and the cross section has been manipulated to include two double-height spaces, one at the front above the parking space and the other overlooking the garden and canal at the lower level. An entrance hall arrives at the circulation zone where a half-flight of stairs leads down to the double-height dining-room, which opens on to the garden and contains a compact kitchen niche. The first floor is occupied by the double-height living space and the second floor by a bathroom and bedroom. The top floor is designated as a work zone with its own external terrace. From the street the elevation is fully glazed with anonymous front and garage doors. From the rear, however, the space is carved away to leave only

Above left The motivating idea behind the design of plot 12 was for the house not to have full frontal views out on to the canal, but rather to make sideways glances. The rear canal elevation has a blank wall with a set-back courtyard; the glazed flank wall allows only views out on to the courtyard and the side of the neighbouring house. *Opposite* Within the context of the other houses this very deliberate approach is quite subversive. *Above right* The bright white bathroom is lit from above. *Opposite below left* The materials of the interior have been reduced to timber and painted metal. *Opposite below right* In the enclosed courtyard space a corner of the floor is folded creating a quirky detail.

the window of the bedroom floating in line with the other buildings two storeys up. The garden space is seen more as an outside room than a traditional courtyard which means that the glass façade of the dining-room is set well back into the plan; the roof of the bedroom becomes the balcony off the work room. Such a sculptural effect is visually arresting and gymnastic. In addition, the materials of the façade – red timber-finished panels – seem to fold into the interior space to become first the ceiling and then the wall of the kitchen.

The success of these two models lies in their provision of a rich series of spaces that can be used in a variety of ways; the ideas may be complicated but the built rooms are full of light and spacious. The architecture is very powerful in defining the volume but not the programme. It is for each occupant to figure out how he or she wishes to inhabit the spaces.

Opposite above From the canal side, plot 18 breaks the solidity of the wall to reveal a set-back garden courtyard. A pop-out window at second-floor level is placed symmetrically above. *Opposite below* From within, the window to the bedroom allows sideways views out. The concrete wall, dark ceiling and timber floor make for a robust interior. *Above left* The double-height space of the living/dining room is divided up by the kitchen which sits neatly in a niche adjacent to the staircase. *Above right* Looking out from the kitchen, the soffit of the floor above frames the view out and adds to the sense of privacy. *Left* Internal windows allow light into the staircase and open up intimate views.

Berman House

New South Wales, Australia, Harry Seidler and Associates

Harry Seidler is arguably Australia's best-known and most venerable architect and has been designing houses for over 50 years. His most recent project, perched on top of a remote sandstone cliff in the Southern Highlands of New South Wales, overlooks a river some 200m (656ft) below. While the base of the building appears to grow out of the craggy landscape, the two white, curved corrugated-metal roof planes float above. From the outside the contrast between the natural rock, which has been made into retaining walls, and the white painted steel suggests a dialogue between nature and artifice. The sinuous but chunky roof forms are supported on thin steel columns with a minimal amount of diagonal bracing. This gymnastic approach is made possible by technological advances in steel manufacturing and certainly would not have been possible when the young Seidler was studying under Walter Gröpius and Marcel Breuer in America. The steel beams were shaped off-site, then clad in corrugated steel in situ.

Following the Modernist tradition the house has been planned with a combination of cellular bedrooms and open-plan living areas in a T-shaped arrangement. Away from the house is a separate garage block, on an axis with a swimming pool cut into the rock behind the house. A rocky path leads to the dark timber front door that opens into the glazed living area. The layout here is a classic arrangement with an island kitchen and dining table in parallel. A fireplace constructed of rough stone mediates between the functional cooking and eating zone and the relaxation area; to one side a fully glazed terrace projects over the cliff to form a vertiginous sun deck facing west. The roof swoops up towards the view and once outside curves down again, protecting part of the terrace and the interior from the strong sun. Chairs and a sofa are formally arranged around the hearth while a single recliner looks out across the valley. The floor throughout is clad in a split grey-coloured stone imported from Norway which contrasts with the rustic sandstone rubble walls, made from rocks found on the site. The palette is monochromatic save for the warmth of the sandstone.

The more private accommodation is reached down a flight of stairs at right angles to a linear courtyard that appears to have been cut into the rock, which in turn is reflected in a slot of water, a reference to the famous courtyard of the Barcelona Pavilion designed by Ludwig Mies van der Rohe in 1929. Underneath this long pool are rainwater storage tanks. On the axis with the stairs is a second chimney stack giving onto a snug area containing sofas and a writing desk. To one side, past a generous dressing-room and bathroom, the main bedroom is accessed, revealing an open glazed corner with views to the rocky walled courtyard and out over the mountains. It too has a fireplace embedded in the east façade. The walls are painted white to match the ceiling and there are no curtains. The detailing of the floor-to-ceiling windows is precise and seamless: there are frames only where the glass slides across, opening onto the balcony. Three more bedrooms, a bathroom and the utility room with its own back door are neatly fitted into the other branch of the 'T' plan.

The owners were keen to make the building as self-sufficient as possible and a number of features contribute to its sustainable operation. Rainwater is collected from the roof, purified and stored in the tanks beneath the house. Water from the swimming pool can be pumped to concealed sprinklers in the roof in the event of a bush fire. Power is generated by solar collectors, and the internal ambient temperature is controlled by opening and closing windows to encourage cross-ventilation.

The overall effect of this house is sculptural; it is an object that has been placed on the top of the hill to catch the light and cast dramatic shadows on to the surrounding terraces. The exterior and interior, including the furniture, have been designed with the same eye and the result is an elegant set piece.

Opposite *Looking up from the river, the cantilevered white balcony and curved metal roof of the Berman House seem to peer over the rocky side of the gorge.*

Above left The steel frame structure and tension rods are visible from the side. The edge of the building appears to hover, ready to retract at any time.
Centre left The main living area is enclosed beneath the giant white wavy roof.
Below left The bedroom enjoys panoramic views out through the glazed corner window; the bed is held between two low built-in cabinets and is seductively covered in fur. *Above* The edge of the sun deck is surrounded by sheets of clear glass making for a vertiginous experience. *Opposite above* The swimming pool has been hollowed out of the rock to create a natural setting for bathing. It also serves as a reservoir in case of bush fires. *Opposite below* The plate-glass window at the end of the living area gives out on to a steep drop below.

Pawson House

London, United Kingdom, Terry Pawson

Architect Terry Pawson has created a house for himself and his family in the south London suburb of Wimbledon. They were already living on the slot site in a house converted from an old stable block but problems with subsidence led Pawson to consider demolishing the building and starting again. At this point he decided that, in order to keep costs down and be as close to the design development process as possible, he would act as the main contractor and involve himself in all aspects of the construction. The result is a house that has a simple enough diagram but is spatially complex, with a surprising number of stairs and level changes, conceived of in cross-section as much as in plan.

The linear site, which also has a considerable drop from street level to the back garden, dictated that the elements of the house be strung along it. The front part of the building is constructed as a timber-framed tower with bedrooms and bathrooms, and from the outside the tall, four-storey façade is an abstract composition of minimally detailed windows and unseasoned oak-board cladding. This is, in part, an acknowlegement of the local suburban Tudor style. To the left-hand side a sliver of space contains the front door, protected by the overhang of the staircase above and offering a discreet way in.

Inside, the space opens up into a three-storey-high entrance hall containing a stark, top-lit, cast-concrete dog-leg stair; it leads up to the bedrooms in the tower and down to the kitchen. From the first floor a linear stair climbs above the front door to the master bedroom on the top floor, which contains a further access stair that pops out onto a roof deck. This is clad entirely in timber, with a trap door from below opening up as though onto the deck of a boat.

Within the entrance hall a void brings borrowed light down to the kitchen. On the axis with the front door is a second door leading to the living areas of the home, a two-storey barrel-vaulted pavilion block constructed in situ from concrete. At the entrance level is the living room, which feels more like a mezzanine deck with its frameless glass balustrade overlooking the dining area and garden below. This room is simply furnished with a long sofa and built-in cabinets, above which is an opening over the timber stairs that continue down along the edge of the building. The lower-ground area, which is some 3m (10ft) below the street, is fully glazed and opens onto an external dining terrace with a lawn beyond. The kitchen has been designed as a U-shaped unit anchored to the back of the staircase wall, clad in pale timber and containing the hob and work surfaces. The opposite wall is lined with full-height cupboards for storage, the refrigerator and the cooker. To the rear is a discreet utility room and access to the main stair of the tower. This part of the home acts as a self-contained living zone united by the robust concrete aesthetic. The barrel vault is a homage to architectural forms used by Le Corbusier in his Maison Jaoul (1956) and later in the Barbican penthouses.

The house itself is a collage of simple architectural forms which are carved up by the staircase slots and voids. The palette of materials is limited to concrete, grey slate, painted white plaster and timber. The detailing appears minimal and the design deals practically with the service spaces. This is a home that has been designed to suit the needs of a family and offers far more flexible accommodation than a Victorian villa. It makes an important contribution to its suburban context, showing how intricate, well-considered, modern architecture can sit well in a traditional streetscape.

Opposite *Partially obscured by trees, the timber-clad tower that houses the bedrooms forms the street façade of Terry Pawson's new suburban house. A large square plate-glass window provides a clue to the programme of the house. The entrance is tucked away to the left below the staircase.*

Above left The roof terrace is clad in timber to resemble the deck of a yacht, including the trap door from below. *Centre left* Stairs to the roof-deck from the master bedroom are compacted into a narrow space. *Below left* Cantilevered from the spine wall, concrete stairs connect the bedrooms with the main family rooms. *Above* The kitchen opens out into an external dining terrace which faces the garden. *Opposite* A cantilevered unit marks the boundary between the kitchen and the dining area but forms only a partial barrier, allowing the spaces to flow into each other.

Parasite House

Rotterdam, The Netherlands, Korteknie and Stuhlmacher Architecten

This bright-green, complicated shape sitting on top of an old warehouse in Rotterdam is an experiment in the construction and siting of new homes. It has been designed by architects Korteknie and Stuhlmacher as part of a cultural programme that aims to create 20 such architectural interventions over the next few years. As such it is a prototype, employing ideas of prefabrication and exploring new sites for domestic inhabitation. This house can 'piggy back' on top of other buildings and structures: the very name, Parasite, suggests a smaller organism that feeds off a larger host. Here PARASITE is an acronymn for Prototypes for Advanced Ready-made Amphibious Small-scale Individual Temporary Ecological houses. The idea is that these structures are almost portable, easy to dismantle and move to other sites if necessary. The facts and figures are impressive; the design process for the 84 sq m (904 sq ft) building took eight weeks, followed by four weeks in the factory. The structure was erected in four days with a further internal finishing period of four weeks.

The building has been conceived as a kit of parts, easily assembled. The whole structure is made entirely out of wood using solid laminated 'Lenotec' panels as its overall construction material. These are cut to size in the factory, where the windows are added, and once assembled in position essential services such as electricity, water and sewage are connected from the existing building. The Lenotec panels are clad in painted plywood.

From the outside Parasite House has a quirky cartoon-like character, completely different from the banal concrete elevator plant room upon which it gingerly perches. It is accessed directly through the top floor of the warehouse and the temporary external

Right Perched precariously on top of a warehouse, the bright-green form of the Parasite House appears alien but friendly. The industrial roofscape of the Rotterdam port area becomes a foil for this imaginative intervention.

stair serves as an emergency exit only. The body of the building is essentially a box with a sheared-off roof, pierced by windows of different shapes and proportions. From a distance its programme is uncertain and it remains enigmatic.

The space within is characterized by the natural unclad timber of the walls, floors and ceiling. Openings and windows have no frames as such and appear to have been punched out of the façade; they are made from fixed double-glazed units. Fresh air is introduced through openable timber shutters. The apparently random arrangement of windows has been designed to maximize the view from this particular location, but could be reconfigured if the building were relocated. A frameless corner window slides open on to a large terrace overlooking the water, which can be used for dining in the summer months. Very few additional surfaces have been added at this stage; the interior literally reflects the materials of

Above Floor-to-ceiling windows frame spectacular views out across the river, while glimpses are afforded through smaller openings. Opposite The Parasite LP2 is a prototype for as many as 20 prefabricated structures of different design and location that will be put up over the next eight to ten years. The programme aims to capture people's imaginations with regard to what constitutes a house and where it can be located.

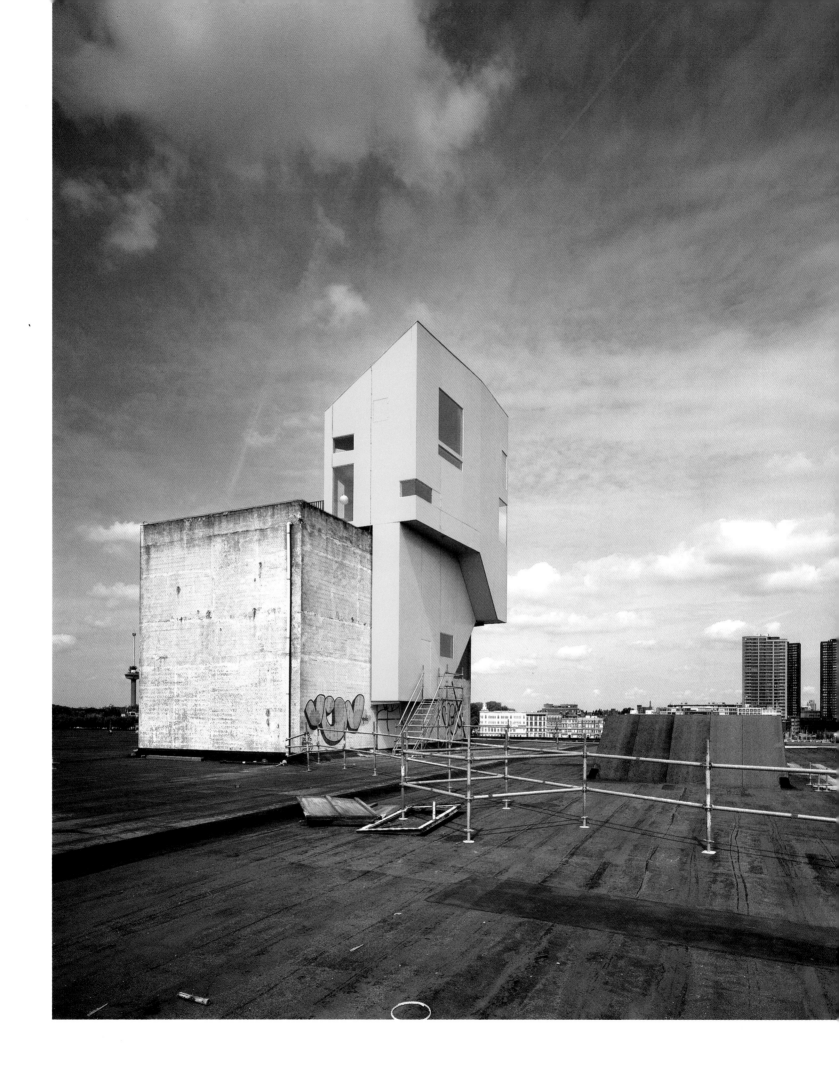

dining in the summer months. Very few additional surfaces have been added at this stage; the interior literally reflects the materials of construction and as a result has the look of a Nordic sauna. The accommodation is simple and well-planned. The 'ground' floor contains a flexible bedroom space, shower room and walk-in closet. A cut-out in the floor creates a visual connection with the floor above and provides spatial interest. The upper floor contains a linear kitchen and the main living area. A solid timber block holds the hob and sink and can be extended to become a fixed table. The volume of the space is characterized by the pitch of the roof, which is left open with a single skylight bringing a shaft of light into the seating area.

As a work-in-progress the house offers a real way forward for the creation of affordable new homes. While in this particular location the building has become something of a landmark, but there is no reason why the parasite cannot be more chameleon-like, blending in with its surroundings if necessary. This new model may not be to everyone's taste, but it represents extraordinarily good value and should be taken seriously as a sustainable proposition for the future of house building.

Top, left to right **During the construction of the Parasite House temporary scaffolding was erected and the prefabricated panels craned into place. The installation of the exterior took only four days.** *Left* **The winding stair connects the flat roof of the factory to the main living space of the house.**

Above   The main living/dining space is located beneath the pitched roof and has the atmosphere of an Alpine ski chalet, not least because of the lack of soft furnishings and the timber-clad, sauna-like environment.

Strawbale House

London, United Kingdom, Sarah Wigglesworth and Jeremy Till

The house and office that architects Sarah Wigglesworth and Jeremy Till built for themselves is an ambitious experiment that tests ideas about sustainability and domesticity using an eclectic palette of materials and construction techniques.

The site is adjacent to a busy railway line and at the time of purchase was home to a working forge. The design for the house was generated from a number of different strands: observations on the nature of a dining table, the centre of the home, where order becomes chaos by the end of a meal; an interest in sustainable technology; and the search for an aesthetic that would not be branded worthy or dull. The result is a highly articulate architectural statement that is a collage of forms, materials and ideas.

From the outside the house is a collection of volumes, which are differently clad or glazed to create a rich three-dimensional object. The building itself can be divided into three elements. The first is a two-storey accommodation block made from timber frames in-filled with straw bales to create super-thick walls, an ancient form of construction that uses the insulating properties of straw. On the outside the straw is protected by corrugated sheeting, the majority of it metal, though a single sheet of transparent polycarbonate allows a sneaky glimpse of the hairy surface behind. Inside, the walls are finished in lime render except for the tiled bathroom, which has a composting toilet.

The main living space, structured predominately around a steel frame, is reached from the bedrooms via a drawbridge at first-floor level. It contains the kitchen and living areas which are divided by a free-form, vertical 'chimney' element that functions as the larder. The insulating property of this brick enclosure coupled with its effect of drawing air through the building from below means that the space is always kept cool. The kitchen has been carefully conceived as an intimate place. The table is fixed and the seating is a timber bench that you have to slide along. It is deliberately reminiscent of being in a boat or caravan; the couple lived on site in a caravan during construction. Within the living area is a steel-framed tower of books, a kind of vertical library, with a staircase that winds up to a trap door giving access to the planted green roof. Further up still is a tiny reading room, somewhere to escape to at the top of the world.

A sliding door at the end of the living space leads to a room holding a large table surrounded by chairs. The key wall is a huge plate-glass window that frames views of the street and the railway line, animated by the dash of speeding trains. When entered from the house this space functions as the dining-room; approached from the other direction, the architects' office, it can act as a conference room. The office block is situated right next to the railway line and has been designed to reduce the impact of noise and vibration. The whole structure sits on springs located at the base of columns clad in gabions, steel-mesh baskets filled with recycled concrete. At ground-level they create an undercroft and a protected entrance for visitors. The walls of the office are clad partly in stacked sandbags full of concrete; over time, as they are exposed to the weather, the bags will rot away leaving a wall of concrete pillows. The side of the building is swathed in a quilted jacket of high-performance fabric which insulates the wall from the weather and the noise.

More than most houses this project demonstrates the inventiveness that can be applied to rethinking the home. Traditional low-tech methods of building – the straw bales and brick larder – have been juxtaposed with sophisticated detailing – the glazed façades and library tower. It is a far cry from the uptight Modernist steel-and-glass boxes to which many still aspire and shows that there is a much richer language available to express domestic inhabitation.

Opposite The Strawbale House and office form a striking contrast to the Victorian terraces in the north London cul-de-sac in which they stand. The railway line runs past on the right.

Left *The straw construction is revealed behind a sheet of clear corrugated polycarbonate while a single column is constructed using an 'as found' tree trunk.* Below left *A galvanized steel frame filled with woven-willow panels forms the boundary between the public realm of the street and the private world of the garden.* Top left to right *Work on the office wing began with the construction of the gabion walls; the wall adjacent to the noisy railway track is made of concrete-filled sandbags and timber railway sleepers are recycled as window surrounds.* Opposite *Beyond the bedroom block, the stripy cantilevered timber box containing the kitchen pokes its head out of the main steel structure of the house. The library tower can be seen beyond.*

Above The office block next to the railway line sits on columns clad in gabions; the columns are placed on springs to absorb the vibrations. *Above right* The eclectic composition of the house gives the sense that the project was constructed over a long period of time and that the design is not meant to be seen as a singular aesthetic, but rather as an appliqué of different building fabrics and techniques. *Right* The kitchen table runs to the outside of the house and is made of fused glass. A glazed door opens up on to a small terrace looking out over the pottager. *Opposite* Perched on piloti, the wedge-shaped façade of the main living space and dining/boardroom is a collage of different windows, solid panels and steel details.

Opus City

Herzebrock, Germany, Drewes and Strenge Architekten

Opus City is the name for a house and warehouse designed by Drewes and Strenge Architekten in Herzebrock, Germany. It was not permitted to build only residential property on the site, so the project was split in two, resulting in a unique programme. Both the clients worked in the fashion industry and had requested a secluded lifestyle, but one which could be subverted on the occasions when they were entertaining and wished to have parties or other gatherings. Certainly from the outside it is not clear quite what kind of building this is. The main street façade is the long arm of the single-storey warehouse building and the construction is of concrete, resulting in a robust retaining wall pierced by an opening with garage doors set back into the recess. The composition suggests domestic use but the visible components are unexpected.

The layout of the plan is a rational L shape. The narrow, rendered, three-storey house is set back into the site, held in place by the interlocking concrete structure of the storage building. The aim was to use strong, industrial materials to make a 'contemporary environment' rather than somewhere cosy or homely. The entrance is on the short side, past an etched-glass corner window that looks into the kitchen area. On the ground floor the main space is open-plan, containing the kitchen, dining and living areas. A stair rises up to the first floor and there is a sculptural dimension to the triple-height space over the dining area. The walls are painted white and the floor is left as concrete, while the metalwork on the bridges and panel details are steely grey, evoking external materials. From here there are views out across an open field to the trees beyond; a pivoting door opens on to a hard-landscaped deck. There are no windows on the side of the house, reinforcing the importance of privacy to the clients.

The solid concrete stair rises up to a landing that bridges the void below and leads to the master bedroom. Here the bed is orientated to look out of a huge picture window across the greenery. At this level there is also a generous bathroom and dressing area. The volumes are simple and it is the empty spaces that make the house intriguing. From the dining table you can look up and see people walking across the bridges at the upper levels. The architects claim that this void occupied by stairs and bridges makes the house feel more spacious and lofty. The top floor of the house has two workrooms or studies and a further bathroom.

In itself the house is not particularly experimental – the carved Cubist spaces are elegant essays in the Modernist style. What is notable is the ingenuity with which both the architects and clients conceived a building that could be constructed in a restricted zone. Thus the language of this hybrid structure is less home and more warehouse, in opposition to so many developments where existing warehouses are turned into homes. The direct relationship between the internal and external language of the architecture results in a bold, uncompromising design.

Opus City is a house that plays with our perceptions: viewed from the street, the building is more about walls and boundaries, repelling interest with its almost boring façade; from the side, the illuminated glass corner and canopied ramp imply a particular kind of inhabitation, but its nature is still unclear; the rear elevation, with its vast expanses of glass, is a completely open composition allowing unobscured views into stark spaces with minimal furnishing. To the visitor, it becomes apparent that the occupants are not interested in living a traditional life and like privacy and control over their environment, which the design of their home elegantly accommodates.

Opposite *The monolithic form of 'Opus City' is punctured by window slots and grooves at the upper level and a small square opening at ground-floor level. The entrance is marked by a cantilevered concrete canopy and ramp as well as the etched-glass corner.*

Above top An axial view through the entrance way reveals the structural games that are being played: the canopy seems to float and a corner made of glass appears to be holding up the weight of the building. *Above* From the street the warehouse elevation is flat and austere until it comes into contact with the edge of the house, where it interlocks with the courtyard wall. *Right* The front door sits underneath a minimalist cantilevered porch.

Right Viewed from the back the rusty metal cladding of the building, with minimal detailing, misleadingly suggests a lifeless programme inside. *Below* The living area looks out on to grass and trees, with the rusted flank wall visible on the left. The void between the two parts of the upper floor opens out above the dining table and is partially filled with two connecting bridges.

Right The open rear elevation is the most private and stretches out away from the road. The geometric articulation creates solids and voids; louvred windows punctuate the white walls and the void areas contain floor-to-ceiling glazing. The result is a precise and well-measured composition.

Machiya Project

Tokyo, Japan, Power Unit Studio, Maruyama Atelier, Akira Yoneda

A cluster of three new houses in Tokyo tells the story of a family who had the idea of developing an urban site to accommodate their growing needs. Two sisters and a brother commissioned a different architect to design a bespoke, jewel-box home for each of them, next door to a house belonging to their parents. Apparently scattered over the site, these buildings form their own family, with a courtyard space in the middle that opens up on to the street. All three buildings are of similar height and have exactly the same site area but are very different in character. Overall the project demonstrates a canny response to the unique opportunity of developing a very precious parcel of land.

The 'C House' was designed for the eldest daughter by Power Unit Studio and is the most box-like. It is planned as an upside-down house, with the sleeping accommodation at ground-floor level in two self-contained bedrooms sharing a common bathroom. A folded metal entrance canopy pierces a plate-glass wall, behind which is the stair, also a folded metal sheet. Next to the entrance on the outside is a single landscape gesture; a cone of earth surrounded by pebbles. This compositional precision continues throughout the building. The main living area, located on the upper floors, reads as a metal beam hovering above the entrance, terminated by an orange book-end wall that moves from the outside into the interior. The stairs rise up within a slot overlooked by the kitchen/dining zone. A plate-glass balustrade provides the necessary protection. At the other end of this linear room is the living space, which ends in the orange wall. Light is brought in via a horizontal skylight running the whole length of the building. Beneath is a huge closet to house all the junk and detritus of everyday life, so that the rest of the house can be left pristine and minimal.

The 'Tea-ory House', owned by the younger daughter, is a far more complex arrangement of forms. The plan has been conceived as a rhombus sitting on top of a rectangle, resulting in a skewed, three-dimensional geometry. It fits together like a puzzle. The south end of the building is a two-storey, dark-coloured fin containing the staircase, with the front door opening off to the side, protected by the overhang of the dining area above. The base of the house is a concrete plinth set above a gravelled landscape. As in the 'C House' there is a bedroom and bathroom at street-level, but more dramatically these have been left open above: looking up from the bed is a view of interlocking white forms which are the balconies of the kitchen at first-floor level. A series of storage niches is carved into the walls around the staircase, which ends in a landing opening up to the kitchen and dining space. Two carefully placed windows, one a diagonal arrow slit and the other a rectangular plane of glass, suggest a very measured response to the surrounding environment. The interior surfaces are a collage of concrete floors, white-painted plaster and dark built-in furniture. Architects Maruyama Atelier have created a very sophisticated and playful house which attempts to maximize the experience of space and complexity of forms by treating the whole as a carved sculptural volume. Although all the buildings have the same footprint, here the total usable floor area is almost half that of the other two.

The third house in this collection, known enigmatically as 'nkm', was designed by Akira Yoneda for the son and his parents. Here three floors have been squeezed in by making use of a clever split section. The plan of the building is essentially square, with a miniature apartment on the ground floor containing a small kitchen, dining-room, bedroom and bathroom. It has its own entrance on the south side and is a compact, neat arrangement.

Opposite A small open courtyard is shared between the three homes that make up Machiya Project. To the right-hand side a conical mound of earth has been planted as part of the minimalist landscaping strategy.

The larger flat has a front door on the north side and is reached via a staircase, which arrives at the kitchen situated on the first floor. The internal arrangement here is curious: a diagonal wall divides off a large bedroom at this level. The bathroom has been designed as a box on the roof reached via an open-tread spiral staircase from the living space. The result is a double-height living zone which has the appearance of somewhere that may have been converted rather than a new building. In this sense it is the most fanciful of the three houses, a highly personal living arrangement which could appear illogical to many people.

Above The brilliant white living and dining space in the C House reads as a balcony overlooking the staircase rising from below. There are no views directly out and the light is brought in at clearstory level. *Opposite* At the opposite end to the kitchen there is a coloured wall. A step leads up on to the deck which screens a linear storage zone.

Above The compact kitchen of the 'nkm' house is fitted into two island units with a stair to the ground floor dipping down the back. A floating spiral stair connects to a bridge leading to the bathroom above. *Right* The south façade is cut away to create the entrance for the ground-floor apartment. This pristine, sculptural block is a finely balanced composition of solid and void.

Above A view from the bedroom of the Tea-ory House looking up at the kitchen shows the complexity of the spatial geometry. A series of cut outs and overlapping planes increases the sense of manipulation.

Right The south façade has a glazed entrance lobby; the form of the skewed living area sits above.

Casa de Blas

Madrid, Spain, Estudio Alberto Campo Baeza

The Casa de Blas is a very good example of a house being better than its diagram might suggest. In this case it is as simple as a box on top of a box. At the site, within the foothills behind Madrid, the terrain is of rocky outcrops scattered with scrubby bushes and trees. The actual location of the house is at the top of a hill which commands views out across the ancient landscape. This kind of rural setting is not obviously idyllic: it is a rougher, readier sort of place, which has not been tamed though agriculture.

The architecture is a forceful response to the aspect and site conditions. As one approaches up the hill, the rough concrete base seems to rise out of the earth and rock around it as a geometric block. The timber shuttering used to create the formwork for the walls has left imprints of woodgrain on the concrete which acts as a mirror to the trees around, a fossilized timber raft. This base is set into the steep hillside so that from above one is almost unaware of the stepping section of the building. On the top of this base sits a pure architectural steel frame, painted white and partly enclosed in glass. The glass walls and door have no visible edges, increasing the sense that the roof is floating. It can be seen as a Modernist paradigm, a reference back to the the purism of Mies van der Rohe. This pavilion functions as a sitting area, protected from the midday sun by the overhanging roof plane. The concrete finish is the same on the inside as the outside. Electric sockets are flushed into the floor so as not to disturb the minimalist aesthetics. An outdoor swimming pool is set into the slab at one end, where you can swim almost to the very edge. This kind of design is deceptively simple: the thin roof of the glass box is achieved by stealthy engineering; the

Right Seen from below, the monolithic rough concrete base of Casa de Blas appears to be embedded in the natural landscape. In contrast the glazed white steel box appears lightweight and pristine.

fact that there are no obvious rainwater pipes is a design secret; and the pool has been carved out leaving all the necessary services hidden out of sight.

A staircase from the deck leads down to the cave-like lower storey. The stair is cut out of the slab as though a trap door has just been opened. The layout below is strangely regimented and symmetrical, reminiscent of monastic cells. The galley kitchen is behind the stair, lit from high-level windows above. On the other side of the linear stair is the main dining and living area, with three punched windows framing views out. On either side are two bedrooms, each with its own bathroom and closet, and a shared fitness room. The ambience inside remains ascetic and pared down. The walls and ceilings are whitewashed; the floor is a sandy stone which turns up the wall to create a flush skirting, a deceptively simple detail when one considers that the function of applied

Above **By night the glass walls almost disappear and the staircase to the house below reads as a glowing slot. The inhabitants can enjoy a 360-degree panorama, although the trade-off is that they themselves can also be seen.**
Opposite above **Assorted square windows are punched into the north wall in an irregular fashion and bring light into the lower ground-floor bedrooms and dining room.** *Opposite below* **From a distance the house looks more like a piece of sculpture than a conventional home.**

skirting is to cover up the sometimes messy detail where a floor meets a wall. It is interesting to note that there are no handrails or railings, suggesting that either the local health and safety regulations have been relaxed or ignored!

In many ways this is a house of extremes and certainly not one that everyone would call home. The design is intellectual and challenging, creating a very rigid framework for inhabitation. There is very much a sense of being on show when out on the deck. This need not be a negative criticism; the simplicity of the house suggests a life free of clutter and possessions. The views out over the countryside are there to be admired and considered in a cerebral manner. In contrast, the presence of the pool and the fitness room suggest the importance of physical well-being. Perhaps, then, this is more of a retreat than a permanent dwelling place, conjuring up a liberating intensity of experience.

Left The staircase to the glass box rises up through the floor without a handrail of any sort. *Opposite above* The glass pavilion is reflected in a swimming pool which is cut into the concrete plinth, emphasizing the ethereal nature of the structure. The water level is exactly flush with the deck. *Opposite below* The living room has a large window directed towards the view. Pale stone floors reflect the light from outside and simple furnishings maintain the simplicity of the building.

Poll House

Although situated on a typical suburban lot in Perth, Western Australia, this is a highly individual building. It comprises two homes, the main one for the owner and his grown-up children and another small flat for the owner's mother. The brief asked that all areas be accessible by wheelchair.

The architect's design strategy was defined by the orientation of the building to gather the maximum amount of daylight. Thus the main living areas face north and the darkest spaces, including the entrance hall and bedrooms, are on the south side. All are orientated towards one of the two central courtyards. From the street a gently sloping, manicured lawn leads down to the low-set, one-storey concrete 'box' topped by an overhanging pitched roof of corrugated metal, characterized by a chunky bull-nosed profile. There is only one long, thin slot window set into this severe composition. The front wall is washed by an even, bright white light set into the soffit, lending an industrial note. This introverted strategy seems more Oriental than New World – until you get inside, where the space seems to stretch out in all directions.

Within, the concrete walls are left clear and all the rooms are arranged as freestanding objects around which flows the circulation. The bathrooms, laundry and guest room are clad in blue-glazed brick while the two bedrooms are of concrete. The more private rooms are clustered around the smaller courtyard while the living and dining spaces look out into the large courtyard. This outdoor space is an essential part of the house: for much of the year it is used for dining and relaxation and has been designed to cast an array of shadows during the day, while at night it is gently illuminated, melting the boundary between inside and out. A simple planting design including a strip of bamboo introduces nature back into the heart of the house.

The white-on-white galley kitchen enjoys views out into the courtyard. The layout is functional and there is generous storage. On the living room side, however, the walls are made of corrugated plastic illuminated from within, apparently dissolving the solidity of the concealed equipment. The furniture, too, has been carefully chosen to add a restrained but sculptural element to the composition.

The architect describes the interior as a landscape of room-sized objects juxtaposed with smaller-scale items such as furniture, low illuminated walls and service rooms, all reflected in the poured-resin floor. One's awareness of materiality is highlighted and animated by sunlight, which casts an intricate shadow across the hallway through the fritted glass of the front door. The bathroom also has a very particular relationship with the outside, as the raised bath, set into a timber-decked plinth, appears to pass through the window to form an external platform. Here too the glass has been etched to allow glimpses out while maintaining a degree of privacy. The walls here are of rough plaster in contrast to the polished surfaces elsewhere in the house.

The declarations of the designer ground the project as a strictly rational one, but an implicit style statement is being made here. From the almost retro curved edge of the roof to the illuminated corrugated walls a hybrid language is being established. There is very little evidence of the detritus of everyday life and yet the overall ensemble is neither clinical nor monastic, the owner's personal art collection adorning many of the concrete walls.

Opposite *From the main courtyard of the Poll House, the living and dining areas are softly illuminated by the translucent kitchen wall and storage unit. The ribbed texture of the roof cladding is echoed by the horizontal back-lit acrylic panels inside. In warm weather, the glazed doors can be slid open to connect the indoor and outdoor spaces.*

Above By night the street façade is illuminated evenly from the soffit. The entrance is marked by a canopy that wraps over the roof to hover above the door and a chunky fin wall of blue-glazed brick shelters the way in; panels containing servicing are attached to the rear side of the wall. *Opposite* The polished walls and floors of the circulation spaces are subtly lit by floor-level lighting, which is also bounced off the curved soffit.

Above The east passage has a curving skylight which casts natural light on to the owner's art collection. The bathroom is denoted by an internal blue-brick wall and has a sliding timber door. Above right The dining and living areas receive daylight from the main courtyard which serves as an outside room, and is an integral part of the home. Centre right Views from the outside reveal the tactile materiality and form of the house. Right A self-contained flat is situated opposite the living areas on the other side of the main courtyard.

Above The glow of the kitchen wall is reflected in the polished floor of the
main living area which is furnished with classic modern furniture. The smaller,
bedroom courtyard is just visible beyond.

Case Study Plans

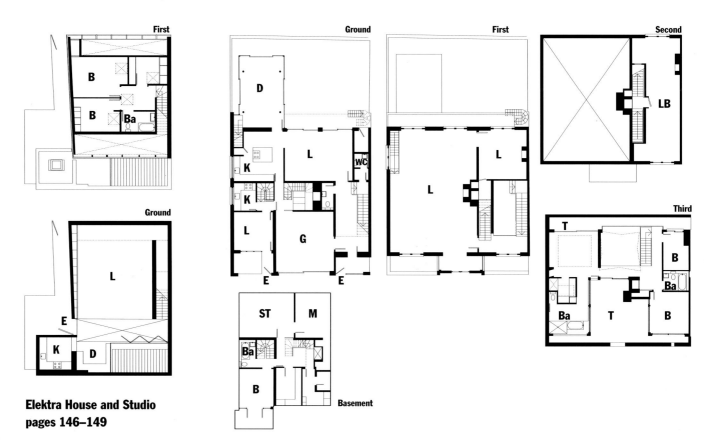

**Elektra House and Studio
pages 146–149**

The Red House pages 156–161

Sheep Farm House pages 150–155

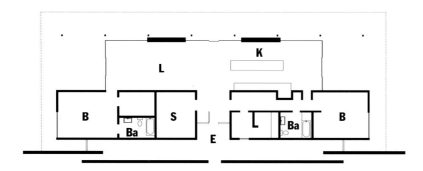

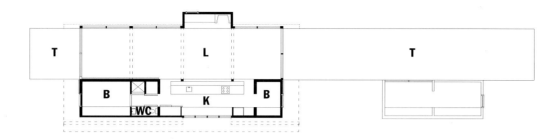

Danielson House pages 162–165

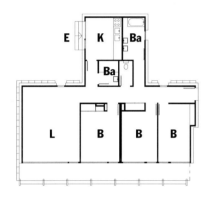

14–19 Rue des Suisses pages 166–169
Typical large apartment

Valley Center House pages 170–175

KEY

B	BEDROOM
Ba	BATHROOM
D	DINING
E	ENTRANCE
G	GARAGE
GY	GYM
K	KITCHEN
L	LIVING
LB	LIBRARY
M	MECHANICAL
O	OFFICE
S	STUDY
ST	STORE
T	TERRACE
WC	WC

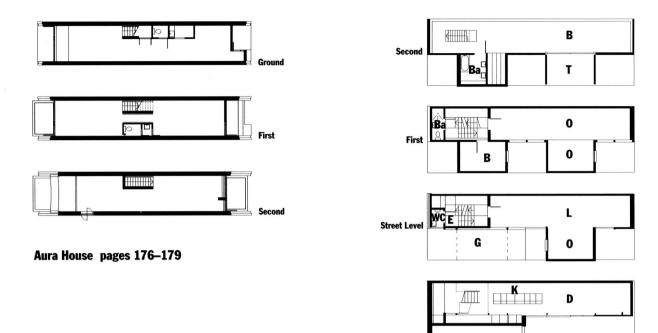

Aura House pages 176–179

**Plot 12, Borneo-Sporenburg
pages 180–185**

Berman House pages 186–189

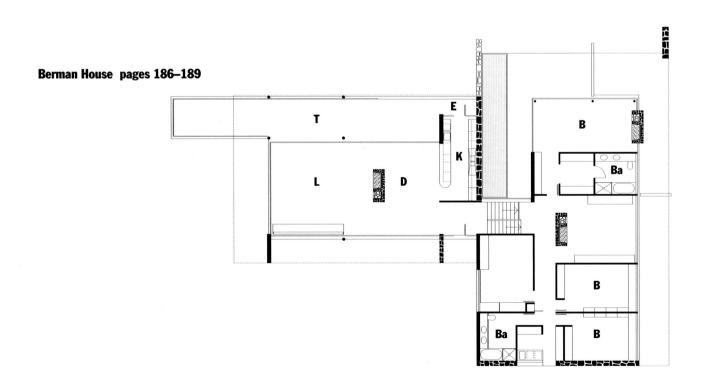

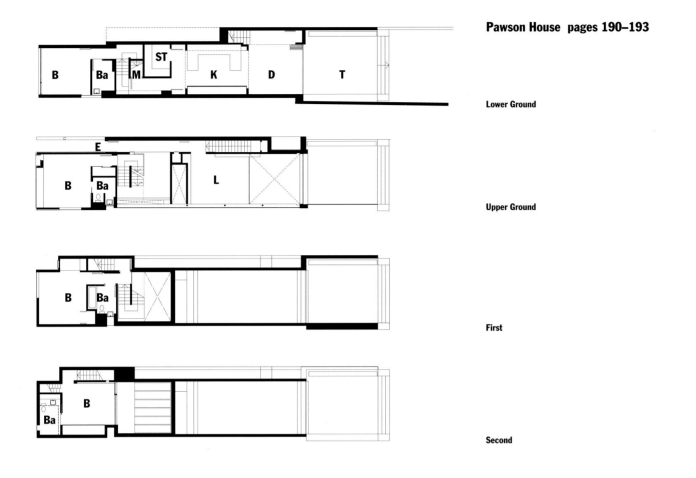

Pawson House pages 190–193

Lower Ground

Upper Ground

First

Second

KEY

B   BEDROOM

Ba   BATHROOM

D   DINING

E   ENTRANCE

G   GARAGE

GY   GYM

K   KITCHEN

L   LIVING

LB   LIBRARY

M   MECHANICAL

O   OFFICE

S   STUDY

ST   STORE

T   TERRACE

WC   WC

Lower

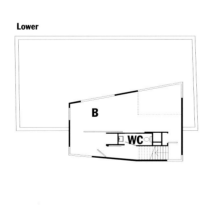

Upper

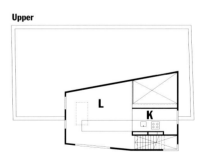

Parasite House pages 194–199

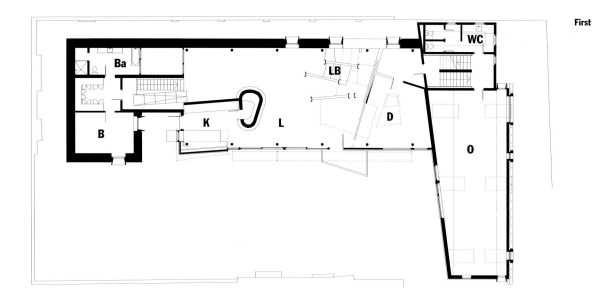

First

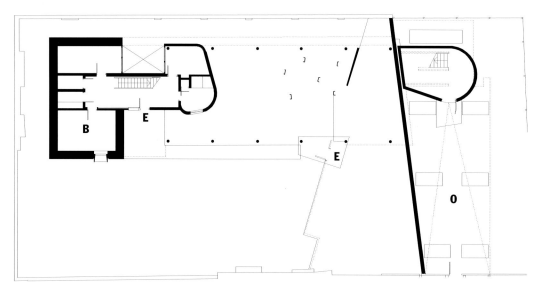

Ground

Strawbale House pages 200–205

KEY

B   BEDROOM

Ba   BATHROOM

D   DINING

E   ENTRANCE

G   GARAGE

GY   GYM

K   KITCHEN

L   LIVING

LB   LIBRARY

M   MECHANICAL

O   OFFICE

S   STUDY

ST   STORE

T   TERRACE

WC   WC

Plans by Paul Clarke

Ground

First

Second

Opus City
pages 206–209

G

Ba

B GY L/D S B

Ground

First

Casa de Blas pages 216–221

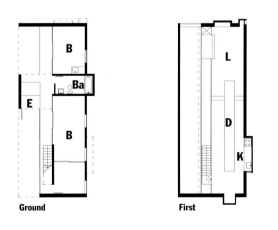

B

Ba

E

B

Ground

L

D

K

First

Machiya Project pages 210–215

Poll House pages 222–227

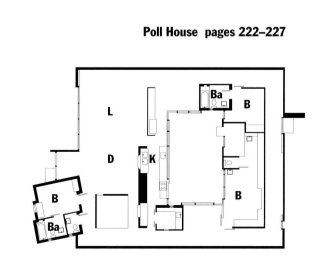

L

Ba

B

D

K

B

B

Ba

B

Contacts

Adjaye/Associates
23-28 Penn Street
London N1 5DL
Tel 020 77394969
Fax 020 77393483

Denton Corker Marshall
49 Exhibition Street
Melbourne
Victoria 3000
Australia
Tel +61 3 9654 4644
Fax +61 3 9654 7870

Tony Fretton Architects
Pegasus House
116-120 Golden Lane
London EC1Y 0TF
Tel +44 20 72531800
Fax +44 20 72531801

Brian MacKay-Lyons
2042 Maynard Street
Halifax
Nova Scotia
Canada B3K 3TU
Tel +1 902429 1867
Fax +1 902 429 6276

Herzog and de Meuron
Rheinschanze 6
CH-4065 Basel
Switzerland
Tel +41 61 385 5758
Fax +41 61 385 57 57

Daly Genik Architects
1558 10th Street
Santa Monica
California 90401
USA
Tel 1 310 656 3180

FOBA
34-3 Tanaka Todo Uji-city
Kyoto
Japan 611 0013
Tel +81 774 20 0787
Fax + 81774 20 9888

MVRDV
Schiehaven 15
3024 EC Rotterdam
The Netherlands
Tel: +31 10 4772860
Fax: +31 10 4773627

Harry Seidler & Associates
2 Glen Street
Milsons Point
NSW 2061
Australia
Tel: +61 2 9922 1388
Fax:+61 2 9957 2947

Terry Pawson Architects
206 Merton High Street
London SW19 1AX
Tel: +44 208 543 2577
 Fax: +44 208543 8677

Korteknie Stuhlmacher Architecten
's-Gravendijkwal 73F
3021 EE Rotterdam
P.O. BOX 25012, 3001 HA
phone +31(0)10 425 94 41
fax +31(0)10 466 51 55

Sarah Wigglesworth Architects
10 Stock Orchard Street
London N7 9RW
Tel: +44 207 607 9200
Fax: +44 207 607 5800

Drewes-Strenge Architekten
Bahnhofstraße 10a
33442 Herzebrock
Germany
Tel: +49 5 245 3208
Fax: +49 5 245 18710

Architectural Produce Association
4-10-20-202 Minami Azabu
Minato-ku
Tokyo 106-0047
Japan
Tel: +81 3 3473 4668
Fax: +81 33473 9653

Alberto Campo Baeza Arquitecto
Almirante 9
28004 Madrid
Spain
Tel/Fax +34 91521 7061

Gary Marinko Architects
M433
Faculty of Architecture,
Landscape and Visual Arts
The University of Western
Australia
35 Stirling Highway
Crawley, WA 6009
Tel: 61 8 9380 2797
Fax: 61 8 9380 1082

Index

Acknowledgements

The publisher would like to thank the following photographers, architects and agencies for their kind permission to reproduce the following photographs in this book:

Front Endpaper Eduard Hueber/archphoto (Architect: Simon Ungers); Back Endpaper Mike McQueen/Impact; 2 Bill Owens; 5 Mechthild Stuhlmacher/Architects: Korteknie & Stuhlmacher; 6 Undine Prohl (Architects: Miquel Adria, Isaac Broid, Michael Rojkind.); 9 Martin Morrell (reproduced by kind permission of Habitat plc and The National Trust); 11 Richard Bryant/Arcaid (Architect: Terry Pawson); 12–13 The British Architectural Library; 14 Sean Sexton Collection/Corbis; 15 G A Duncan/Mary Evans Picture Library; 16 National Trust Photo Library; 17 Robert Estall/Corbis; 18 William Cooper/World of Interiors; 19 Richard Bryant/Arcaid © DACS 2003; 20 Country Life Picture Library (Architect: EdwardLutyens); 21 above Chicago Historical Society (Architect: Frank Lloyd Wright) © ARS, NY and DACS, London 2003; 21 centre Frank Lloyd Wright Foundation © ARS, NY and DACS, London 2003; 21 below Paul Rocheleau; 22 Hunterian Art Gallery, University of Glasgow (Architect: Charles Rennie Mackintosh); 23 Bridgeman Art Library (Architect: Josef Hoffmann); 24 The British Architectural Library (Architect: Antoine Gaudi); 25 The British Architectural Library (Architect: Le Corbusier) © Fondation Le Corbusier and DACS 2003; 26 above David Churhill/Arcaid (Architect: Le Corbusier/P Jeanneret) © Fondation Le Corbusier and DACS 2003; 26 centre and below Mark Luscombe-Whyte/The Interior Archive (Architect: Le Corbusier) © Fondation Le Corbusier and DACS 2003; 27 Thomas A Heinz/Corbis (Architect: Gerrit Rietveld); 28 Soenne, Aachen; 29 Museum of Finnish Architecture (Architect: Alva Aalto); 30 The British Architectural Library; 31 Hedrich Blessing (Architect: Ludwig Mies van der Rohe) © DACS 2003; 32 Paul Rocheleau (Architect: Phillip Johnson); 33 Julius Shulman; 34 Max Dupain/courtesy of Harry Seidler & Associates; 35 Bettman/Corbis (Architect: Minoru Yamasaki); 36 above Rollin R. LaFrance/courtesy of Venturi, Scott Brown and Associates, Inc; 36 below courtesy of Gwathmey Siegel & Associates; 37 Timothy Hursley (Architect: Frank Gehry & Associates); 38 Hans Werlemann (Architect: Office for Metropolitan Architecture); 38–39 Christian Richters (Architect: Van Berkle & Bos); 40–41 Undine Prohl (Architects: Miquel Adria, Isaac Broid, Michael Rojkind.); 42 Anthony Crolla/World of Interiors; 43 Bill Batten/World of Interiors (Architect: Claudio Silvestrin); 44 right Undine Prohl (Architects: Miquel Adria, Isaac Broid, Michael Rojkind.); 44 above and below left Verne Fotografie (Architect: Haat & Ivan); 45 Sue Barr/View (Architects: Dow Jones); 46 Undine Prohl (Architects: Miquel Adria, Isaac Broid, Michael Rojkind.); 47 Christian Richters (Architects: Herzog and de Meuron); 48 left Timothy Hursley (Architect: Wendell Burnett); 48 right Christian Richters (Architects: Mecanoo Architects); 49 Hiroyuki Hirai (Architect: Shigeru Ban); 50 Christian Richters (Mecanoo Architects); 51 Toshi Kobayashi (Architects: FOBA); 52 Timothy Hursley; 53 Jun Takagi (Sejima Architects); 54 Ryuji Miyamoto/courtesy of Bolles Wilson Architects; 55 above Hiroyuki Hirai (Architect: Kei' Ichi Irie / Power Unit Studio / Producer: Masahiro Ouchi / Architectural Produce Association); 55 below Shoichi Ono (Architect: Kei' Ichi Irie / Power Unit Studio, Structural designer: Masahiro Ikeda / MIAS Producer: Masahiro Ouchi / Architectural Produce Association); 56 James Mortimer/World of Interiors (Architects: Hudson Architects); 57 Tohru Waki (Architect: Katsuyasu Kishigami); 58 Christian Richters (Architect: Frank Drewes); 59 Hélène Binet/Arcblue (Architect: Caruso St John); 60 above Vega MG; 60 below Richard Davies (Architects: 51% Studios); 61 Andrew Lee (McKeown Alexander Architects); 62-63 Adrian Taylor (FAT Architects); 64 Timothy Hursley (Architect: Wendell Burnett); 66–67 Jeff Walls /courtesy of Lacoste & Stevenson Architects; 68 Tonkin-Liu Architects; 69 Tim Brotherton (Hudson Featherstone Architects); 70 Andre Rival (Architects: Peter Herle & Werner Stoll); 70 above Christian Richters (Architects: MVRDV); 70 below Andre Rival (Architect: Peter Herle and Werner Stoll); 71 Christian Richters (Architect: Dirk Jan Postel; 73 Timothy Hursley (Architect: Wendell Burnett); 74 Yoshio Shiratori (Architect: Takayama & Amorphe); 75 Jun Takagi (Architect: Takayama & Amorphe); 76 Living etc/IPC magazines (Architect: Joe Hagan); 77 left Hiroyuki Hirai (Architect: Akira Voneda / Architecton / Producer: Masahiro Oushi / Architectural Produce Association);77 centre Shoichi Ono (Architect: Akira Yoneda); 77 right Courtesy of Architecture Studio; 79 Edmund Sumner (Thinking Space Architects); 80 Ed Reeve/Red Cover (Architect: William Russel); 81 Tim Griffith (Architects: Ivan Rijavec); 82 Margherita Spiluttini (Architect: Eichinger Oder Knechtl); 83 Jacques Dirand/Maison Madame Figaro (Architect: Mark Guard); 84 Smoothe/Courtesy of Percy Conner Architects; 85 Courtesy of Phillippe Gazeau Architects; 86–87 Bill Timmerman(Architect: Rick Joy); 88–89 Timothy Hursley (Architect: Marlon Blackwell); 90-91 Christoph Mäckler (Prof Dieter Leistner/Architect: Prof Christoph Mäckler); 92–93 Philippe Ruault (Architect: Lacton-Vassal); 94 Nicholas Kane/Arcaid (Niall McLaughlin Architects); 95 Jussi Tiainen (Architect: Olavi Koponen); 96 Giorgio Possenti/Vega MG; 97 Timothy Hursley (Architect: Sam Mockbee); 98–99 Richard Davies

(Architect: Seth Stein); 100–101 Henning Larsen (Jens Lindhe/Architect: Henning Larsens Tegnestue); 102 Sue Barr/View (Dow Jones Architects); 103 David Churchill/Arcaid (James Gorst Architects); 104 Aage Lund (Dombernowsky & Christensen Architects); 105 Friedrich Busam/Architekturphoto (Architect: Roberto Briccola); 106 Timothy Hursley (Architect: Marlon Blackwell); 107 Richard Davies (Architect: Future Systems); 109 Amy Eckert (Architect: Preston T Phillips); 110 Ray Joyce (Architect: Craig Rosevar); 111 above Earl Carter/Taverne Agency (Architect: Denton Corker Marshall); 111 centre Reiner Blunck Fotodesign; 111 below Earl Carter/Taverne Agency (Architect: Denton Corker Marshall); 112–113 Undine Prohl (Architect: Brian MacKay-Lyons); 114 Jussi Tiainen (Architect: Jyrki Tasa); 115 Ivan Terestchenko (Architect: Eric Gouesnard); 116–117 Hans Werlemann (Architect: MVRDV); 118–119 Ray Main/Mainstream; 120 Alan Bishop/Alamy; 121 Christian Richters (Neutelings Riedijk Architects); 122 above left and right andcentre left Andy Keate (Walter Menteth Architects); 122 below Peter Bonfig (Architect: GAS-Sahner Architekten BDA); 124 above Keith Hunter Photography (Architects: Page and Park); 124 centre Keith Hunter Photography (Architects: Richard Murphy); 124 below Keith Hunter Photography (Architects: Page and Park); 125 Keith Hunter/Arcblue (Elder & Cannon/Rick Mather Architects); 127 Paul Raferty/View (Architect: Edouard François); 128 Eric Sierins/courtesy of Harry Seidler & Associates; 129 John Gollings (Renzo Piano); 131 Peter Korrak (Architect: Coop Himmelbau/Jean Nouvel); 132 Michael Moran (Architect: Diller and Scofidio); 133 above Keith Collie (Architect: de Architeckten Cie); 133 below Jeroen Musch(Architect: de Architeckten Cie); 134 Peter Durant/Arcblue; 135 Bill Owens; 136–137 Richard Waite; 138 Jeff Minton Photography; 139 Raf Makda (Architects: Cartright Pickard); 141 left Tim Soar (Architects: AHMM); 141 right James Morris/Axiom Photographic Agency (Architect: Georg Briendl); 142 Charlotte Wood/Arcblue (Architect: Proctor Matthews); 143 above Charlotte Wood/Arcblue (EPR Architects Ltd); 143 below Raf Makda/View (Bill Dunster Architects); 144–145 Tim Griffith (Architects: Denton Corker Marshall); 147–149 Lyndon Douglas (Architect: Adjaye/Associates); 150–151 Reiner Blunck (Architect: Denton Corker Marshall); 151 centre Tim Griffith (Architect: Denton Corker Marshall); 151 below Reiner Blunck; 152–154 below Reiner Blunck (Architect: Denton Corker Marshall); 154–155 Tim Griffith (Architect: Denton Corker Marshall); 155 below left and right Reiner Blunck (Architect: Denton Corker Marshall); 157 Peter Durant/Arcblue (Tony Fretton Architects); 158–161 Hélène Binet/Arcblue (Tony Fretton Architects); 161 below Peter Durant/Arcblue (Tony Fretton Architects); 163–165 Undine Prohl (Architect: Brian MacKay-Lyons); 167–169 Paul Raferty/View (Architects: Herzog & de Meuron); 171–175 Undine Prohl (Daly Genik Architects); 176–179 Tohru Waki/Shokokusha Pub Ltd (Architect: FOBA); 180–181 The Japan Architect (Architect: MVRDV); 182–185 Nicholas Kane (Architect: MVRDV); 187–189 Max Dupain/courtesy of Harry Seidler & Associates; 191–193 Richard Bryant/Arcaid (Terry Pawson Architects); 194–195 Anne Bousema (Architects: Korteknie & Stuhlmacher); 196 Errol Sawyer (Architects: Korteknie & Stuhlmacher); 197 Mechthild Stuhlmacher(Archietcts: Korteknie & Stuhlmacher); 198 above Rien Korteknie (Architects: Korteknie & Stuhlmacher); 198 below Anne Bousema (Architects: Korteknie & Stuhlmacher); 199 left Rien Korteknie (Architects: Korteknie & Stuhlmacher); 199 right Anne Bousema (Architects: Korteknie & Stuhlmacher); 201 Paul Smoothy (Architects: Sarah Wigglesworth & Jeremy Till); 202 above left Philip Bier/View (Architects: Sarah Wigglesworth & Jeremy Till); 202 above right and below left Paul Smoothy (Architects: Sarah Wigglesworth & Jeremy Till); 203 below Paul Smoothy (Architects: Sarah Wigglesworth & Jeremy Till); 204 left Philip Bier/View (Architects: Sarah Wigglesworth & Jeremy Till); 204 right and 205 Paul Smoothy (Architects: Sarah Wigglesworth & Jeremy Till); 207–209 Christian Richters (Frank Drewes Architect); 211 Hiroyuki Hirai (Architects: Kei' Ichi Irie/Power Unit Studio, Hiroshi Maruyama/Marayama Atelier, Ayira Yoneda/Architecton. Producer: Masahiro Ouchi/Architecture Produce Association); 212 Shoichi Ono (Architect: Kei' Ichie Irie/Power Unit Studio); 213 Hiroyuki Hirai (Architect: Kei' Ichie Irie/Power Unit Studio); 214 above Shoichi Ono (Architect: Akira Yoneda/Architecton); 214 below Hiroyuki Hirai (Architect: Akira Yoneda/Architecton); 215 above Shoichi Ono (Architect: Hiroshi Maruyama/Maruyama Atelier); 215 below Hiroyuki Hirai (Architect: Hiroshi Maruyama/Maruyama Atelier); 216–221 Alberto Emanuele Piovano (Architect: Alberto Campo Baeza); 223–227 Jacqueline Stevenson (Architect: Gary Marinko)

Every effort has been made to trace the copyright holders, and we apologise in advance for any unintentional omissions and would be pleased to insert the appropriate acknowledgements in any subsequent publication.

The author wishes to thank:

Matthew Barac, Iain Borden, Hilary Burden, Terence and Vicky Conran, Richard Doone, Roz Diamond, Lucy Gowans, Bridget Hopkinson, Marissa Keating, Lee Mallett, Fred Manson, Paul Monaghan, Morag Myerscough, Rose Pipes, Alicia Pivaro, Jane Rendell, Alastair Soane, Liz Soane, Vicky Thornton, Sarah Wigglesworth, Jane Zara.